BASIC JAPANESE
CONVERSATION
DICTIONARY

BASIC JAPANESE CONVERSATION DICTIONARY

*(English-Japanese
Japanese-English)*

Revised and Enlarged

by

SAMUEL E. MARTIN

Professor of Far Eastern Linguistics
Yale University

CHARLES E. TUTTLE CO.
Rutland, Vermont
Tokyo, Japan

Published by the Charles E. Tuttle Company, Inc.
of Rutland, Vermont & Tokyo, Japan
with editorial offices at
Suido 1-chome, 2-6, Bunkyo-ku, Tokyo

Copyright in Japan, 1957
by Charles E. Tuttle Co., Inc.

Library of Congress Catalog Card No. 57-8797

International Standard Book No. 0-8048-0057-X

First printing, 1957
Second printing, 1958
Second edition (revised
and enlarged), 1959
Seventy-fifth printing, 1989

Printed in Japan

CONTENTS

Introduction vii

Part I
  English-Japanese 3

Part II
  Japanese-English 129

Part III
  Writing Charts. 263

Part IV
  Money Conversion Tables 269

INTRODUCTION

This dictionary has a purely practical aim. That is to put you into immediate communication with Japanese who speak little or no English. You will find 3000 useful English words with their most common Japanese equivalents. Only the most frequent meanings of the English words have been included; naturally, each English word has many other meanings. But the chances are, the meaning you want is the one given here. When the Japanese equivalent is a verb, it is given in the polite present form: -mas' "does" or "will do." From this form the polite past and the polite suggestion forms are easily made: -mash'ta "did" or "has done"; -mashō "let's do" or "I think I'll do." In parentheses are given the PLAIN present form (-u or -ru), and the gerund (-te or -de "doing" or "does and"). From the gerund, you can make the plain past tense by changing -te or -de to -ta or -da. Some English adjectives correspond to Japanese nouns, and these fall into two categories: ordinary nouns, which link to a following noun with the word no; and copular nouns, which link to a following noun with the word na. Copular nouns are shown in this dictionary by adding **na** in parentheses: **genki (na)**. Ordinary nouns are sometimes given with **no** in parentheses to show they correspond to English adjectives but are not copular nouns.

Some of the words are preceded by three dots. This means that you put in front of them the words that would come after the corresponding English. For example English "in" would be followed by, let us say, "America." But the corresponding Japanese word **ni** would be preceded by **Amerika**: "in America" would be **"Amerika ni."**

If you have trouble pronouncing the Japanese words, just look up the English word you want to express, and point to the Japanese writing. Your Japanese friend will then be able to figure out what you are trying to say. If you can't find the word you want, try to think of some other common English word that means the same thing, and look that up. If it isn't in the dictionary either, then try using the English word right in the middle of your Japanese.

The Japanese is presented in a slightly modified form of the Hepburn romanization. Most of the consonants are pronounced about as in English, the vowels as in Italian: **a** as in f*a*ther, **e** as in m*e*t or y*e*s, **i** as in mar*i*ne or macaron*i*, **o** as in s*o*lo or

Pogo, **u** as in r*u*le or L*u*lu. These vowels are shorter than our English vowels; the long varieties (marked **ā, ō, ū, ii,** and either **ei** or **ē**) are a little longer and tenser than the English sounds like them. In everyday speech, many final long vowels are shortened. The apostrophe (as in **s'koshi arimas'**) represents a short **u** (after **s, k,** etc.) or **i** (after **sh, ch**) which is suppressed in ordinary speech. You will find **s'** alphabetized as if it were **su, sh'** as if it were **shi** You may hear other vowels suppressed occasionally. The tongue is pushed farther forward (against the teeth) for Japanese **t, d,** and **n** than for the English sounds. The Japanese **r** may sound like a combination of **r, l,** and **d** to you. Your English **d** (if you say it very quickly) is probably the closest. But don't mix it up with a Japanese **d!** The Japanese **g** never has the "soft" *j*-sound as in *g*em or *g*in; it is either "hard" as in *g*et or *g*ift or it has the "ng" sound in sin*g*er. If you have trouble with the "ng" version, forget it and use the "hard" **g** everywhere. The **n** which comes at the end of a word sounds a little bit like a weak "ng" instead of a full-fledged **n;** try to imitate this if you hear the difference.

In the Japanese-English part, the Japanese verbs are presented both in the polite present (**-mas'**) and the plain present (**-u** or **-ru**). When the two forms would come

ix

close together in alphabetical order, they are given on one line; in other cases, you will find two entries.

The beginner will find he can take the Japanese equivalents of English words (skipping the little, unimportant English words) and string them together much as he does in English. The Japanese will understand him most of the time, even though the effect is choppy. If you want to find out more about how to put the words together in sentences, you will find it useful to get the author's other two works, EASY JAPANESE and ESSENTIAL JAPANESE. This dictionary should be a useful supplement for students using these two textbooks.

In order to make this book a handy size it was necessary to restrict the number of words and the amount of explanatory materials included. The author would be happy to hear of any omissions which particularly trouble you as you use the book.

PART I

English-Japanese

NOTE : The Japanese equivalents are given both in Romanization and in native writing. If you wish, you can find the English word you want to communicate and point to the Japanese equivalent, letting your Japanese friends pronounce it themselves. In the Romanized part, each verb is given in the polite present (**-mas'**) with the plain present (**-u**) and the gerund (**-te**) following in parentheses. In the native writing only the plain present is given. This is the form in which the verbs appear in Japanese dictionaries.

A

a, an *see* one (*but usually omitted in Japa- | *nese*)

abacus **soroban** そろばん

abandon **s'temas'** (*s'teru, s'tete*) 捨てる

abbreviate **ryaku-shimas'** (*-su, -sh'te*) 略す

abbreviation **ryakugo** 略語

abhor *see* hate

ability **sai** 才

able *see* can

abolish **haishi shimas'** (*suru, sh'te*) 廃止する

abortion **datai** 堕胎

about (a certain amount) **yaku** ... 約 *or*
... **gurai** ぐらい; *see also* almost, around

about (a certain time) ... **goro** (**ni**) ごろ (に)

about (*concerning*) ... **ni tsuite** (**no**) につい
て (の)

(talk) about ... (**no**) **koto o iimas'** (*yū,*
itte or yutte) の事を言う

above ... (**no**) **ue** (**ni**) (の) 上 (に)

abroad **gaikoku** (**de**) 外国 (で)

abrupt **totsuzen** 突然

absent **rusu** (*des'*) 留守 (です)

absent-minded **bon-yari shimas'** (*suru, sh'te*)
ぼんやりする

absolutely **honto ni** ほんとに

absurd **baka-rashii** ばからしい

abuse *see* scold

A.C. current **kōryū** 交流

accent **ak'sento** アクセント; *see also* pronunciation, dialect

accept **moraimas'** (*morau, moratte*) 貰う

accessible (*easy to get to*) **iki-yasui** 行きやすい

accident **jiko** 事故 *or* **dekigoto** 出來事

accidentally **gūzen ni** 偶然に

accomodations (*place to stay*) **tomaru tokoro** 泊まる所

accompany (...to) **issho ni ikimas'** (*iku, itte*) (と)一緒に行く; **o-tomo shimas'** (*suru, sh'te*) お供する

accomplish (sh'te) **shimaimas'** (*shimau,* しまう (して) しまって)

according to ...**ni yoru to** によると

account (*bill*) **kanjō** 勘定

(on) account of *see* because

accountant **kaikei** 会計

accumulate (*it accumulates*) **atsumarimas'** (*atsumaru, atsumatte*) 集まる; (*accumulates it*) **atsumemas'** (*atsumeru, atsumete*) 集める

accurate **seikaku (na)** 精確 (な)

accuse **hinan shimas'** (*suru, sh'te*) 非難する

accustom oneself to ...**ni naremas'** (*nareru, narete*) に慣れる

ache **itamimas'** (*itamu, itande*) 痛む

acid **san (no)** 酸 (の)

acknowledge **mitomemas'** (*mitomeru, mitomete*) 認める

acquaintance **shiriai** 知り合い

acquainted with ...**o shitte imas'** (*iru, ite*) を知つている

acquire *see* get

4

across ... (no) **mukō ni** (の) 向うに

act *see* do

action, activity **katsudō** 活動

activity (*agency*) **kikan** 機関

actor **haiyū** 俳優

actress **joyū** 女優

actually **jitsu wa** 実は *or* **jitsu ni** 実に

acute (*sharp*) **surudoi** 鋭い; (*severe*) **hageshii** 烈しい; (*sudden*) **kyūsei** (no) 急性 (の)

ad *see* advertisement

add **kuwaemas'** (*kuwaeru, kuwaete*) 加える

additional *see* more

address **tokoro** 所; (*house number*) **banchi** 番地; (*written*) **tokoro-gaki** 所書き *or* ate-adequate *see* enough ⌞**na** 宛名

adhesive tape **noritsuki-têpu** のり付きテープ

adjacent *see* next

adjective **keiyōshi** 形容詞

adjoining **tonari** (no) 隣 (の) ⌜整える

adjust **totonoemas'** (*totonoeru, totonoete*)

administration (*of government*) **gyōsei** 行政

admirable **migoto** (na) 見事 (な)

admiral **taishō** 大将; (vice) **chūjō** 中将; (rear) **shōshō** 少将 ⌜感心する

admire **kanshin shimas'** (*suru, sh'te*)

admit (*lets in*) **iremas'** (*ireru, irete*) 入れる; (*acknowledges*) **mitomemas'** (*mitomeru, mitomete*) 認める; (*confesses*) **uchi-akemas'** (*-akeru, -akete*) 打ち明ける

5

adolescence **shishunki** 思春期

adolescent **seinen** 青年

adopt (*a boy*) **yōshi ni shimas'** (*suru, sh'te*)
養子にする; (*a girl*) **yōjo ni shimas'**
(*suru, sh'te*) 養女にする

adopted (son) **yōshi** 養子; (daughter) **yōjo** 養女

adore *see* love

adult **otona** 大人

advance **susumimas'** (*susumu, susunde*) 進む
(in) advance **sono mae ni** その前に

advantage **toku** 得; (take ...of) **riyō shimas'**
(*suru, sh'te*) 利用する

adventure **bōken** 冒険

adverb **f'kushi** 副詞

advertisement **kōkoku** 広告

advice **sōdan** 相談 *or* **chūkoku** 忠告

adviser (*consultant*) **komon** 顧問

aerial *see* antenna

affair **koto** 事 *or* **jiken** 事件

affect *see* influence

affected **kidotta** 気取つた

affection **aijō** 愛情

affliction **kurushimi** 苦しみ

afford (**jūbun na**) **kane ga arimas'** (*aru,
atte*) (十分な) 金がある

afraid (of ...) (... **ga**) **kowai** こわい

Africa **Afurika** アフリカ

after (... **no**) **ato de** 後で

afternoon **hiru kara** 昼から *or* **gogo** 午後

6

after-shave (lotion) **as'torinzen** アストリンゼン

again **mō ichi-do** もう一度 *or* **mō ik-kai** 「もう一回

against (*in contrast to*) **...ni taish'te** に対して; (*opposing*) **...ni hantai sh'te** に反対して; (*running into*) **...ni butsukatte** にぶつかって

age **toshi** 年

agency (*middleman*) **dairi** 代理; (*organization*) **kikan** 機関

agent **dairi** 代理; (*ticket agent*) **kippu-uri** 切符売り

aggravating **haradatashii** 腹立たしい

aggression **shinryaku** 侵略

ago **...mae ni** 前に

agony **kurushimi** 苦しみ

agree **sansei shimas'** (*suru, sh'te*) 賛成する

agriculture **nōgyō** 農業

ahead **saki (ni)** 先(に)

aid *see* help

ail *see* sick

aim at **neraimas'** (*nerau, neratte*) 狙う

air **kūki** 空気

air base **kūgun-kichi** 空軍基地

air conditioning **reibō** 冷房

airfield *see* airport

air force **kū-gun** 空軍

air mail **kōku-bin** 航空便

airman **kōkū-hei** 航空兵

airplane **hikōki** 飛行機

airport **hikōjō** 飛行場

7

airsick(ness) **hikō-yoi** 飛行酔い

aisle **tsūro** 通路

à la carte **ippin-ryōri** 一品料理

alarm clock **mezamashi-dokei** 目ざまし時計

album (*photograph*) **shashin-chō** 写真帳;
(*stamp*) **kitte-chō** 切手帳

alcohol **arukōru** アルコール

alike **onaji** 同じ

alive **ikite imas'** (*iru, ite*) 生きている

all **minna** 皆 *or* **zembu** 全部

alley **yokochō** 横町

Allies **Rengō-koku** 連合国

allow **yurushimas'** (*yurusu, yurush'te*) 許す

allowance (*bonus*) **teate** 手当て

almost **hotondo** ほとんど

alone **hitori (de)** 一人(で)

along... ...**no doko ka (de)** のどこか(で)

alongside ...**no soba** のそば

aloud **koe o dash'te** 声を出して

alphabet (*English*) **ē-bii-shii** エービーシー;
already **mō** もう ⌊(*Japanese*) **kana** かな

also ...**mo** も *or* **sono ue** その上

altar **saidan** 祭壇 *or* **seitaku** 聖卓

alter **naoshimas'** (*naosu, naosh'te*) 直す

alternately **kawaru-gawaru** かわるがわる

alternating current *see* AC

although ...**no ni** のに

altogether **minna de** 皆で

aluminum **arumi(nyūmu)** アルミ(ニューム)

alumnus (of . . .) (. . . no) shusshin (の) 出身

always itsu mo いつも

am see is

. . . a.m. gozen . . . 午前

amateur amachua アマチュア

ambassador taishi 大使

amber kohaku こはく

ambition (*hope*) netsubō 熱望; (*energetic spirit*) haki 覇気

ambulance kyūkyūsha 救急車

America Amerika アメリカ or Beikoku 米国

American (person) Amerika-jin アメリカ人 or Beikoku-jin 米国人

ammunition dan-yaku 弾薬　「(内, 間)

among . . . no naka (*or* uchi *or* aida) の中

amount to (how much) (ikura) ni narimas' (*naru, natte*) (いくら)になる

ample see enough

amusement asobi 遊び

amusing omoshiroi おもしろい

an see a

analysis bunseki 分析

ancestor senzo 先祖

anchor ikari 錨

ancient mukashi no 昔の or kodai no 古代の

and . . . (*if you are including each item*) . . . to と; (*if you are choosing typical items*) . . . ya や

(does) and shi *or* VERB GERUND (-te form)

(is) and **shi** *or* ADJECTIVE GERUND (**-k'te form**)

angel **tenshi** 天使

angle **kakudo** 角度; (*scheme*) **kufû** 工夫

(gets) angry **okorimas'** (*okoru, okotte*) 怒る

animal **dôbutsu** 動物

ankle **ashi-kubi** 足首

anklets **sokkusu** ソックス

annex **bekkan** 別館

anniversary **kinembi** 記念日

announce (*inform*) **shirasemas'** (*shiraseru, shirasete*) 知らせる

announcer **anaunsā** アナウンサー

annoying **urusai** うるさい

another **mô hitotsu** もうひとつ

answer **kotaemas'** (*kotaeru, kotaete*) 答える

ant **ari** あり

antenna **antena** アンテナ

anthropology **jinrui-gaku** 人類学

anti-American **haibei** (**no**) 排米(の)

antibiotic(s) **taikinsei-yakuzai** 対菌性薬剤

anticipate **machimas'** (*matsu, matte*) 待つ

anti-Communist **hankyō** (**no**) 反共(の)

antidote **dokkeshi** 毒消し

antifreeze **kōtōketsu-zai** 抗凍結剤

anti-Japanese **hannichi** (**no**) 反日(の)

antique **jidai-mono** 時代物

antiseptic **bôfu-zai** 防腐剤

anxious *see* worried

any *usually omitted in Japanese*

anybody **hito** 人
anybody (at all) **dare de mo** 誰でも
anyhow (*nevertheless*) **to-ni-kaku** とにかく
anyhow (at all) **dō de mo** どうでも
anyone *see* anybody
anyplace *see* anywhere
any time **itsu de mo** いつでも 「*ten omitted*)
anything (*something*) **nani ka** 何か (*but of-*
anything (at all) **nan de mo** 何でも
anyway *see* anyhow
anywhere (*somewhere*) **doko ka** どこか
anywhere (at all) **doko de mo** どこでも
apartment **apāto** アパート
apiece **...zutsu** ずつ
apologize **wabimas'** (*wabiru, wabite*) 詫びる
apparatus **sōchi** 装置
appear **miemas'** (*mieru, miete*) 見える
appetite **shokuyoku** 食欲
apple **ringo** りんご
application (*for job, etc.*) **mōshi-komi** 申込み
appointment *see* date
appreciate **arigataku omoimas'** (*omou, omot-*
te) ありがたく思う 「*zuite*) 近づく
approach **chikazukimas'** (*chikazuku, chika-*
approve **sansei shimas'** (*suru, sh'te*) 賛成する
approximately **daitai** 大体
April **Shi-gatsu** 四月
architecture **kenchiku** 建築
are *see* is

11

argument **kenka** けんか

arm **te** 手 or (*strictly*) **ude** 腕

army **rikugun** 陸軍

around (...no) **mawari ni** まわりに; *see also*
「about

arrangements **jumbi** 準備

arrive (at)(ni) **ts'kimas'** (*ts'ku, tsuite*)(に)着く

art **bijutsu** 美術 or **geijutsu** 芸術

article (*thing*) **mono** 物; (*write-up*) **kiji** 記事

as (*like*) (...no) **yō (ni)** (の)様 (に)

ashamed **hazukashii** はずかしい

ashes **hai** 灰

ash tray **hai-zara** 灰皿

ask (a person a question) (...ni) **kikimas'**
(*kiku, kiite*) (に)聞く

ask (a favor of a person) (...ni ...o) **tanomimas'** (*tanomu, tanonde*) たのむ or
negaimas' (*negau, negatte*) 願う

association **kyōkai** 協会　　「*at*) ...**de** で

at (*being located at*) ...**ni** に; (*happening*

athlete **senshu** 選手

Atlantic Ocean **Taiseiyō** 大西洋

atmosphere (of a place) **fun-iki** ふんいき

atom **genshi** 原子

atombomb **genshi-bakudan** 原子爆弾

attach **ts'kemas'** (*ts'keru, ts'kete*) 付ける

attack **kōgeki shimas'** (*suru, sh'te*) 攻撃する

attention **chūi** 注意

auditorium **kōdō** 講堂

Australia **Ōs'torariya** オーストラリヤ

Australian (*person*) Ōs'torariya-jin オースト

average **heikin** 平均 Lラリヤ人

avoid **sakemas'** (*sakeru, sakete*) 避ける

awake **mezamemas'** (*mezameru, mezamete*)

(go) away **ikimas'** (*iku, itte*) 行く L目ざめる

(take) away **torimas'** (*toru, totte*) 取る

awful **osoroshii** 恐ろしい

B

baby **aka-chan** 赤ちゃん *or* **akambo** 赤んぼ

bachelor **dokushin** 独身 *or* **hitori-mono** 独身者

back (*behind*) **ushiro** うしろ

back (*of body*) **senaka** 背中

bad **warui** 悪い *or* **dame** だめ

bag **fukuro** 袋

baggage **te-nimotsu** 手荷物

bake **yakimas'** (*yaku, yaite*) 焼く

bakery, bakeshop **pan-ya** パン屋

ball **tama** たま *or* **mari** まり

bamboo **take** 竹

bamboo shoots **takenoko** 筍

bandage **hōtai** 繃帯

bank **ginkō** 銀行

bar **saka-ba** 酒場 *or* **bā** バー

barber(shop) **tokoya** 床屋

base (*military*) **kichi** 基地

baseball **yakyū** 野球

basket **kago** 籠 *or* **zaru** ざる

bath, (takes a ...) **furo** (ni hairimas'; *hairu, haitte*) 風呂 (に入る)

bathing suit **mizugi** 水着

bathroom (*for bathing*) **furo-ba** 風呂場; (*toilet*) **benjo** 便所

battery **denchi** 電池

be *see* is

beach **hama** 浜

bean **mame** 豆

bear (*animal*) **kuma** 熊

beard **hige** ひげ

beat *see* hit; *see* win

beautiful **utsukushii** 美しい

beauty parlor **biyōin** 美容院

because...... **kara** から *or* ...**tame** ため

become ...**ni narimas'** (*naru, natte*) になる

bed **toko** 床; (*American*) **shindai** 寝台

bedroom **ne-ma** 寝間 *or* **shinshitsu** 寝室

bee **mitsu-bachi** 密ばち

beef **gyūniku** 牛肉

beefsteak **bif'teki** ビフテキ

beer **biiru** ビール

before (...**no**) **mae** (**ni**) (の)前(に)

beggar **kojiki** 乞食

begin (*it begins*) **hajimarimas'** (*hajimaru, hajimatte*) 始まる; (*begins it*) **hajimemas'** (*hajimeru, hajimete*) 始める

behind (...**no**) **ushiro** (**ni**) (の)うしろ(に)

believe **shinjimas'** (*shinjiru, shinjite*) 信じ

る; *see also* think 「(*doorbell*) **beru** ベル

bell (*large*) **kane** かね; (*small*) **rin** りん;

belong (to) (...**ni**) **zoku-shimas'** (*-suru*, *-sh'te*) (に) 属する

below (...**no**) **sh'ta** (**ni**) (の) 下 (に)

belt **bando** バンド *or* **obi** 帯

bend (*it bends*) **magarimas'** (*magaru*, *magatte*) 曲る; (*bends it*) **magemas'** (*mageru, magete*) 曲げる

beneath *see* below

beside (...**no**) **tonari** (**ni**) (の) となり (に) *or* (...**no**) **waki** (**ni**) (の) 側 (に)

besides **sono ue ni** その上に

best **ichiban ii** 一番いい

bet **kakemas'** (*kakeru, kakete*) かける *or* **kake o shimas'** (*suru, sh'te*) かけをする

better **motto ii** もっといい *or* ...**yori ii** ...よりいい

between (...**no**) **aida** (の) 間

beyond (...**no**) **mukō** (の) 向う

Bible **Seisho** 聖書

bicycle **jitensha** 自転車

big **ōkii** 大きい

bill **kanjō** 勘定

billiards **tama-ts'ki** 玉突

bird **ko-tori** 小鳥 *or* **tori** 鳥

birthday **tanjōbi** 誕生日

bit (*a little*) **s'koshi** 少し

bite **kamimas'** (*kamu, kande*) 咬む *or* **kami-ts'kimas'** (*-ts'ku, -tsuite*) かみつく

bitter **nigai** にがい

15

black **kuroi** 黒い

blanket **mōfu** 毛布

blemish **kizu** きず

blind **mekura** めくら

blindfold **mekakushi** 目隠し

blink **ma-tataki** (*or* **ma-bataki**) **shimas'** (*suru, sh'te*) またたき (まばたき) する

blister **mizu-bukure** 水ぶくれ

blizzard **fubuki** 吹雪

block *The closest Japanese equivalent is* **chōme,** *a square which includes several blocks. For distances, use* -**chō**: It is three blocks from here. **Koko kara san-chō des'.**

blond **kimpatsu** 金髪

blood **chi** 血

bloom **sakimas'** (*saku, saite*) 咲く

bloomers **mompe** モンペ

blot, bloch **shimi** しみ

blotter **suitori-gami** 吸取紙

blouse (*of uniform*) **jaketsu** ジャケツ; (*women's, children's*) **burausu** ブラウス; (*coat*) **uwagi** 上着

blow **f'kimas'** (*f'ku, fuite*) 吹く

blowfish **fugu** ふぐ

blue **aoi** 青い

blueprint **ao-jashin** 青写真

blunt (*dull-edged*) **kirenai** 切れない; (*dull-pointed*) **nibui** 鈍い; (*rude*) **busahō** (**na**) 無作法 (な)

16

blush **akaku narimas'** (*naru, natte*) 赤くなる

board **ita** 板

boast **jiman shimas'** (*suru, sh'te*) 自慢する

boat **fune** 船 or (*small one*) **kobune** 小舟

bobby soxer **jogak'sei** 女学生

bock beer **kuro-biiru** 黒ビール

body **karada** 体

(gets) bogged (down) **iki-zumarimas'** (*-zumaru, -zumatte*) 行き詰る

boil (on skin) **haremono** はれもの

boiled water (*cooled for drinking*) **yu-zamashi** 湯ざまし 「かし; (*pot*) **kama** かま

boiler (*for heating water*) **yu-wakashi** 湯わ

boils (water) **o-yu o wakashimas'** (*wakasu, wakash'te*) お湯を沸かす

(water) boils **o-yu ga wakimas'** (*waku, wa-ite*) お湯が沸く

boisterous **yakamashii** やかましい or **sawa-gashii** さわがしい

bold **daitan** (na) 大謄(な) 「or -tan 反

bolt (*of door*) **kannuki** 閂; (*of cloth*) **-maki** 巻

bomb **bakudan** 爆弾

bomber **bakugeki-ki** 爆撃機

bombing **bakugeki** 爆撃

bond (*debenture*) **saiken** 債券

bone **hone** 骨

bonfire **takibi** 焚火

bonito **katsuo** かつお

bonus **shōyo(-kin)** 賞与(金)

17

book **hon** 本
bookcase **hombako** 本箱
bookends **hon-tate** 本立て
bookie **kakeya (san)** 賭け屋（さん）
bookkeeping **boki** 簿記
bookmark **shiori** しおり
bookshelf **hon-dana** 本棚
bookshop **hon-ya** 本屋
boom (*prosperity*) **keiki** 景気; (*fad*) **būmu**
　ブーム; (*sound*) **don** どん
booster (*of current*) **shōatsu-ki** 昇圧機
booth (*selling things*) **baiten** 売店; (*telephone*)
　denwa-shitsu 電話室
boots **naga-gutsu** 長靴
border (*edging*) **heri** へり; (*of district, etc.*)
　kyōkai 境界; (*of country*) **kokkyō** 国境
boring (*dull*) **taikutsu (na)** 退屈（な）「生れる
(is) born **umaremas'** (*umareru, umarete*)
borrow **karimas'** (*kariru, karite*) 借りる
bosom **futokoro** ふところ
boss **shujin** 主人
both **ryōhō** 両方 *or* **dochira mo** どちらも
bother **mendō** 面倒 *or* **meiwaku** 迷惑
bothersome **mendō-kusai** 面倒臭い
bottle **bin** びん
bottle opener **sennuki** 栓抜き
bottom **soko** 底　　　　　　　「はずむ
bounce **hazumimas'** (*hazumu, hazunde*)
bound (for) **...e ikimas'** (*iku, itte*) へ行く

18

bound (to) **kitto ...(suru) deshō** きっと(する)でしょう

bouquet **hanataba** 花束

bourbon **burubon** ブルボン

bow (*of head, etc.*) **ojigi** (**o shimas'**; *suru, sh'te*) お辞儀(をする)

bow (*shooting or violin*) **yumi** 弓

bowel movement **daiben** (**shimas'**; *suru, sh'te*) 大便(する)

bowl **chawan** 茶碗

bowl(ful) **-hai** 杯 (1 **ip-pai**, 2 **ni-hai**, 3 **sam-bai**)

bowlegged **gani-mata** がにまた or **wani-ashi** わに足

box **hako** 箱

boxing **kentō** 拳闘 or **bokkushingu** ボックシング

box office **kippu uriba** 切符売り場

boxtree **tsuge** つげ

boy **kodomo** 子供 or **otoko no ko** 男の子 or **bōya** 坊や or **botchan** 坊ちゃん

bracelet **ude-wa** 腕輪

brag about **jiman shimas'** (*suru, sh'te*) 自慢する or **hokorimas'** (*hokoru, hokotte*) 誇る

braid **amimas'** (*amu, ande*) 編む

brains **nō-miso** 脳味噌 or **atama** 頭

brakes **burēki** ブレーキ or **wa-dome** 輪止め

branch (*of tree*) **eda** 枝; (*of store*) **shi-ten** 支店; (*of rail line*) **shi-sen** 支線

brass **shinchū** 真鍮

brassiere **burajia** ブラジア or **burā** ブラー

brave **yūkan** (**na**) 勇敢(な)

brazier **hibachi** 火鉢

Brazil **Burajiru** ブラジル

bread **pan** パン or **shoku-pan** 食パン

bread crumbs **pan-ko** パン粉

break (*it breaks*) **kowaremas'** (*kowareru, kowarete*) こわれる; (*breaks it*) **kowashimas'** (*kowasu, kowash'te*) こわす

breakable **koware-yasui** こわれやすい

breakfast **asa-han** 朝飯

(sea) bream **tai** たい

breast (*chest*) **mune** 胸; (*woman's*) **chichi** 乳

breathe **iki o shimas'** (*suru, sh'te*) 息をする

breechcloth **fundoshi** ふんどし

breeches *see* trousers

breeze *see* wind

brewery **jōzōsho** 醸造所

bribe **wairo** わいろ

brick **renga** 煉瓦

bride **hana-yome** 花嫁

bridegroom **hana-muko** 花婿

bridge **hashi** 橋

bridle **baroku** 馬勒

brief *see* short

brief case **kaban** かばん

brigade **ryodan** 旅団

brigadier general **dai-shō** 代将 or **jun-shō** 準将

bright **akarui** 明るい

bring (*a thing*) **motte kimas'** (*kuru, kite*) 持って来る; (*a person*) **tsurete kimas'** (*kuru, kite*) 連れて来る

20

Britain *see* England

British *see* English

brittle **moroi** 脆い

broad *see* wide

broadcast **hōsō** (**shimas'**; *suru, sh'te*) 放送

broadcasting station **hōsō-kyoku** 放送局

brocade **nishiki** 錦

broil **yakimas'** (*yaku, yaite*) 燒く

broken (*not working*) **dame des'** だめです
  or **koshō shimash'ta** 故障しました

brokenhearted **shitsuren** 失恋

broker **naka-gai** 仲買 *or* **naka-dachi** 仲立

brook **ogawa** 小川

broom **hōki** 箒

bronze **seidō** 青銅

brothel **jorō-ya** 女郎屋

brother **otoko no kyōdai** 男のきょうだい;
  (*older brother*) **nii-san** 兄さん *or* **ani** 兄;
  (*younger brother*) **otōto** (san) 弟(さん)

brow (*eyebrow*) **mayu** まゆ; (*forehead*) **hitai**
  ひたい

brown **cha-iro** (no) 茶色 (の)

brown bread **kuro-pan** 黒パン

bruise **uchi-kizu** 打ちきず

brush **burashi** ブラシ *or* **hake** はけ; (*for
  writing or painting*) **fude** 筆

Brussels sprouts **me-kyabetsu** 芽キャベツ

brutal **zankoku** (na) 残酷 (な)

bubble **awa** 泡 *or* **abuku** あぶく; (*soap*)
  shabon-dama シャボン玉

21

bubble gum **fūsen-gamu** 風船ガム

bucket **baketsu** バケツ or **oke** 桶

buckle **shime-gane** 締金

buck private **heisotsu** 兵卒

bucktooth **soppa** 反歯

buckwheat (noodles) **(o-)soba** (お)そば

bud *(of leaf)* **me** 芽; *(of flower)* **tsubomi** 蕾

Buddha **Hotoke-sama** 仏様; *(statue of)*

Buddhism **Bukkyō** 仏教　└**Butsu-zō** 仏像

Buddhist priest **bōzu** 坊主 or **sōryo** 僧侶

Buddhist temple **(o-)tera** (お)寺

buddy *see* friend

budge *see* move

budget **yosan** 予算

bug **mushi** 虫

bugle **rappa** らっぱ

build **tatemas'** *(tateru, tatete)* 建てる

building **tatemono** 建物 or **birujingu**

(light) bulb **denkyū** 電球　└ビルジング

bulge **fukurami** 脹らみ

(in) bulk **bara de** ばらで　┌地均し

bulldozer **burudōza** ブルドーザ or **ji-narashi**

bullet **tama** たま or **dangan** 弾丸

bulletin board **keiji-ban** 掲示板

bum **rumpen** ルンペン

bump (into) **...ni butsukarimas'** *(butsukaru, butsukatte)* にぶつかる　┌でこぼこ

bump *(swelling)* **kobu** 瘤; *(in road)* **dekoboko**

bunch *(cluster)* **fusa** 房; *(pile)* **yama** 山;

22

(*bundle*) **taba** 束; (*group*) **mure** 群

bundle **tsutsumi** 包み

bunion **soko-mame** 底豆

bureau (*department*) **kyoku** 局; (*chest*) **tansu** 「たんす

burglar **dorobō** 泥棒

burlesque **s'torippu** ストリップ

Burma **Biruma** ビルマ

burn (*it burns up*) **yakemas'** (*yakeru, yakeie*) 焼ける; (*burns it up*) **yakimas'** (*yaku, yaite*) 焼く; (*fire burns*) **moemas'** (*moeru, moete*) 燃える 「げっぷ(を出す)

burp **geppu** (**o dashimas'**; *dasu, dash'te*)

burst (*it bursts*) **yaburemas'** (*yabureru, yaburete*) 破れる; (*bursts it*) **yaburimas'** (*yaburu, yabutte*) 破る

bury **umemas'** (*umeru, umete*) 埋める

bus **basu** バス

bush **kamboku** 灌木

business (*job*) **shigoto** 仕事

business (*enterprise*) **jitsugyō** 実業; (*commerce*) **shōgyō** 商業

business (*errand, etc.*) **yō** 用 *or* **yōji** 用事

businessman **jitsugyōka** 実業家

bust *see* burst

busy **isogashii** 忙しい

but **sh'kashi** しかし *or* **keredomo** けれども *or* ...(des') **ga** です(が)

butcher (shop) **niku-ya** 肉屋

butt (*cigarette*) **suigara** 吸い殻

23

butter **batā** バター
butterfly **chō** *or* **chōchō** 蝶(々)
buttocks **shiri** 尻　　　　「ボタン(をかける)
button **botan** (*o kakemas'; kakeru, kakete*)
buy **kaimas'** (*kau, katte*) 買う
by (*not later than*) **...made ni** までに
by means of **...de** で

C

cab *see* taxi
cabaret **kyabarē** キャバレー
cabbage **kyabetsu** キャベツ
cable (**kaigai**) **dempō** (海外)電報
cactus **saboten** さぼてん
cafe (*coffee shop*) **kōhii-ten** コーヒー店;
　(*restaurant*) **ryōri-ten** 料理店
cage (*for birds*) **kago** 籠; (*for animals*) **ori** 檻
cake **kēki** ケーキ; (*Japanese*) **o-kashi** お菓子;
　(*spongecake*) **kas'tera** カステラ
calamity **sainan** 災難
calendar **koyomi** 暦
calisthenics **taisō** 体操
call **yobimas'** (*yobu, yonde*) 呼ぶ
calligraphy **shodō** 書道
calling card **meishi** 名刺
calling-card case **meishi-ire** 名刺入れ
callus **tako** たこ　　　　　　「平気で
calm(ly) **ochitsuite** おちついて *or* **heiki de**

camel **rakuda** らくだ
camera **shashinki** 写真機
camp **kyampu** キャンプ
campus **kōtei** 校庭
can (*tin*) **kan** 鑵
can (*is able*) **dekimas'** (*dekiru, dekite*) 出来る;
  (*suru*) **koto ga dekimas'** (する)事が出来る
Canada **Kanada** カナダ
Canadian **Kanada-jin** カナダ人
canary **kanariya** カナリヤ
cancel (**tori-**)**keshimas'** (*kesu, kesh'te*) (取)消す
cancer **gan** がん
candle **rōsoku** ろうそく
candy **o-kashi** お菓子
candy store **kashi-ya** 菓子屋
cane **s'tekki** ステッキ
canned goods **kanzume** 鑵詰
cannon **taihō** 大砲
can opener **kan-kiri** 鑵切り
canvas (*material*) **zukku** ズック
cap *see* hat
cape (*of land*) **misaki** 岬
capital (*city*) **shufu** 首府
capital (*money*) **shihon** 資本
capitalism **shihon-shugi** 資本主義
capitalist **shihon-ka** 資本家
capsule **kapuseru** カプセル
captain (*army*) **tai-i** 大尉; (*navy*) **tai-sa** 大佐
car **kuruma** 車; **jidōsha** 自動車

caramel **kyarameru** キャラメル

carbarn **shako** 車庫

carbolic acid **sekitan-san** 石炭酸

cardboard **bōru-gami** ボール紙

cards **torampu** トランプ

care **yōjin** 用心

career **shokugyō** 職業

(is) careful **ki o ts'kemas'** (*ts'keru, ts'kete*)

carp (*fish*) **koi** 鯉

carpenter **daiku** 大工

carpet **jūtan** or **kāpetto** カーペット

carrot **ninjin** 人参

carry **motte ikimas'** (*iku, itte*) 持って行く

(hand)cart **te-guruma** 手車 or **kuruma** 車

carton *see* box

cartoon **manga** 漫画

carve **kizamimas'** (*kizamu, kizande*) 刻む or
  horimas' (*horu, hotte*) 彫る

carving **horimono** 彫物

case (*circumstance*) **ba(w)ai** 場合;(*box*) **hako** 箱

cash (on hand) **gen-nama** 現なま

cash (a check, etc.) **genkin ni hiki-kaemas'**
  (*-kaeru, -kaete*) 現金に引換える

cash (a large bill) **komakaku shimas'** (*suru,*
cashbox **kane-bako** 金箱 ⌊*sh'te*) 細かくする

cashier **kanjō-gakari** 勘定係

cask **taru** 樽

cast (*of play*) **yakuwari** 役割り

castle (o-)**shiro** (お)城

26

casual **nanige-nai** 何げない

cat **neko** 猫

catalog **mokuroku** 目録; (*directory*) **meibo** 「名簿

catch **torimas'** (*toru, totte*) 取る

caterpillar **kemushi** 毛虫

catfish **namazu** なまず

Catholic **Katorikku** カトリック

cattle **ushi** 牛

cause (*of an effect*) **moto** 元 or **gen-in** 原因;
  (*reason*) **wake** わけ or **riyū** 理由; (*purpose*)
  tame 為 「**seru, sasete**」にさせる

cause (someone to do) **...ni sasemas'** (*sa-*
cautious **yōjim-bukai** 用心深い

cave **hora(-ana)** ほら(穴)

cedar **sugi** 杉

ceiling **tenjō** 天井

celebrate **iwaimas'** (*iwau, iwatte*) 祝う

celery **serori** セロリ

cellar **chika-shitsu** 地下室

cement **semento** セメント

cemetery **hakaba** 墓場 or **bochi** 墓地

censor(ship) **ken-etsu** 検閲

cent **sento** セント

center **mannaka** まん中

centimeter **senchi(-mētoru)** センチ(メートル)

centipede **mukade** むかで

century **hyaku-nen** 百年 or **seiki** 世紀

ceremony **shiki** 式

certain **tash'ka(na)** 確か(な)

certainly **mochiron** 勿論

cesspool **osui-dame** 汚水だめ or **gesui-dame**

Ceylon **Seiron** セイロン

chain **kusari** 鎖(くさり)

chair **isu** 椅子

chalk **chōku** チョーク

chance **chansu** チャンス

change (*it changes*) **kawarimas'** (*kawaru, kawatte*) 変る; (*changes it*) **kaemas'** (*kaeru, kaete*) 変える (換える，替える); (*changes trains, etc.*) **nori-kaemas'** (*-kaeru, kaete*) 乗り換える

change (*small money*) **komakai** (*kane*) こまかい(金); (*money returned*) **o-tsuri** お釣

character (*quality*) **seishitsu** 性質; (*personal traits*) **seikaku** 性格

charcoal **sumi** 炭

charcoal brazier *see* brazier

charge (how much) (**ikura**) **shimas'** (*suru, sh'te*) いくらする

charity **hodokoshi** 施し

charm (*good-luck piece*) **o-mamori** お守り

(is) charming **miryoku ga arimas'** (*aru, atte*) 魅力がある 「かける

chase **oi-kakemas'** (*-kakeru, -kakete*) 追い

chaser **ato-nomi** 後飲

chaste **teisetsu** (*na*) 貞節 (な) 「立話

chat **sekem-banashi** 世間話 or **tachi-banashi**

chatter **shaberimas'** (*shaberu, shabette*) 喋る

chatterbox **oshaberi** おしゃべり

chauffeur **untenshu** 運転手

cheap **yasui** 安い

cheat **damashimas'** (*damasu, damash'te*)

check (*bank*) **kogitte** 小切手; (*baggage*)
    ⌊**chikki** チッキ

checkers (*Japanese*) **go** 碁

checkroom **azukari-jo** 預り所

cheek **hoppeta** ほっぺた

cheerful **kigen ga ii** 機嫌がいい

cheese **chiizu** チーズ

cheesecloth **kanreisha** かんれいしゃ

chef *see* cook

chemistry **kagaku** *or* **bake-gaku** 化学

cherry (tree) **sakura** さくら (桜); (*fruit*)
    sakurambo さんらんぼ

cherry blossoms **sakura no hana** さくらの花

chest (*of body*) **mune** 胸; (of drawers) **tansu**
    たんす   ⌈焼ぐり

chestnut **kuri** くり (栗); (*roasted*) **yaki-guri**

chew **kamimas'** (*kamu, kande*) かむ

chicken **tori** 鳥 *or* **niwatori** 鶏

chief (*head*) **chō** 長 *or* **chōkan** 長官; (*principal*) **shuyō** (**na**) 主要(な) *or* **omo** (**na**) 主(な)

child **kodomo** 子供 *or* **ko** 子

childhood **kodomo no toki** 子供の時

chill(y) *see* cold

chimney **entotsu** 煙突

chin **ago** あご

China **Chūgoku** 中国

Chinese (*person*) **Chūgoku-jin** 中国人

Chinese character **kanji** 漢字

chip (*of wood*) **koppa** こっぱ; (*crack*) **kizu** きず

chisel **nomi** のみ

chlorine **enso** 塩素

chocolate **chokorēto** チョコレ

chocolate malt **choko-moruto** チョコモルト

chocolate milk **choko-miruku** チョコミルク

choir **kōrasu** コーラス

choke (*he chokes*) **iki ga tsumarimas'** (*tsumaru, tsumatte*) 息が詰る; (*chokes him*)
... **no iki o tomemas'** (*tomeru, tomete*)

cholera **korera** コレラ ⌐の息を止める

choose **erabimas'** (*erabu, erande*) 選ぶ

chop *see* cut

chopping board **manaita** まないた

chopstick rest **hashi-oki** 箸置き

chopsticks **o-hashi** お箸

chow *see* food

chow mein **yaki-soba** 焼そば

Christ **Kiris'to** キリスト

Christianity **Kiris'to-kyō** キリスト教

Christmas **Kurisumas'** クリスマス

chrysanthemum **kiku** きく (菊)

church **kyōkai** 教会 ⌐*soda pop*

"cider" **saidā** サイダー (*a very fizzy lemon*

cigar **shigā** シガー *or* **hamaki** 葉巻

cigarette case **tabako-ire** たばこ入れ ⌐吸口

cigarette holder **paipu** パイプ *or* **suikuchi**

cigarettes **tabako** たばこ

cinch **wake mo nai (koto)** 訳もない (事)

30

cinder **moegara** 燃がら

cinema *see* movies

cinnamon **nikkei** 肉桂

circle **maru** 丸 *or* **en** 円

circulate (*it circulates*) **mawarimas'** (*mawaru, mawatte*) 廻る; (*circulates it*) **mawashimas'** (*mawasu, mawash'te*) 廻す

circumstance **ba(w)ai** 場合 *or* **koto** 事

circus **sākasu** サーカス *or* **kyokuba** 曲馬

city **machi** 町

civilian **shimin** 市民　　「**heijō-f'ku** 平常服

civilian clothes, civies **fudan-gi** 不断着 *or*

civilization **bummei** 文明 *or* **bunka** 文化

clan **uji** 氏　　　　「**te o tatakimas'**

clap (hands) **te o tatakimas'** (*tataku, tataite*)

class **kurasu** クラス *or* **kyū** 級

classroom **kyōshitsu** 教室　　「はさみ

claw (*of animal*) **tsume** 爪; (*of crab*) **hasami**

claw hammer **kuginuki** 釘抜き

clay **nendo** 粘土

clean **kirei (na)** きれい (な); (*cleans it*) **sōji shimas'** (*suru, sh'te*) 掃除する 「リーニング

cleaning (*dry*) **dorai-kuaiiningu** ドライ・ク

clear (*bright*) **akarui** 明るい; (*understood*) **wakatta** 解った; (*easy to see*) **mi-yasui** 見やすい; (*easy to understand*) **wakari-yasui** 解りやすい; (*unimpeded*) **jama ga nai** じゃまがない

clearly (*distinctly*) **hakkiri** はっきり

clerk (*in shop*) **ten-in** 店員; (*in office*) **jimu-in** 事務員

clever **rikō (na)** 利口 (な)

cliff **gake** 崖

climate **kikō** 気候

climb **noborimas'** (*noboru, nobotte*) 上る

clippers (*barber's*) **barikan** バリカン

clock **tokei** 時計

clockwise **migi-mawari (ni)** 右廻りに

clogs *see* wooden shoes

close **shimemas'** (*shimeru, shimete*) 締める

close *see* near

closet **oshi-ire** 押入れ

cloth **orimono** 織物; (a piece of) **kire** きれ

clothes **kimono** 着物; (American) **yōf'ku** 洋服; (Japanese) **waf'ku** 和服

clothesbag **sentaku-ire** 洗濯入れ

clothesbrush **kimono-burashi** 着物ブラシ

clothesline **mono-hoshi** 物干し

cloud **kumo** 雲

(gets) cloudy **kumorimas'** (*kumoru, kumotte*) 曇る

cloves **chōji** 丁子

club (*social group or card suit*) **kurabu** クラブ; (*stick*) **kombō** 棍棒; (*golf club*) **uchi-bō** 打棒

clue **itoguchi** いとぐち

clumsy **heta (na)** 下手 (な) *or* **bukiyō (na)** 不器用 (な)

cluster *see* bunch

coach (*railroad*) **kyaku-sha** 客車; (*athletic*) **kōchi** コーチ

coal **sekitan** 石炭

coal mine **tankō** 炭坑

32

coast **kaigan** 海岸

coat **uwagi** 上着; (overcoat) **gaitō** 外套

coax **odatemas'** (*odateru, odatete*) おだてる

cobweb **kumo no su** (*or* **ito**) くもの巣(糸)

cockroach **abura-mushi** 油虫

cocktail (party) **kakuteru** カクテル

cocoa **kokoa** ココア

coconut **yashi** やし

cocoon **mayu** まゆ

cod(fish) **tara** 鱈

co-ed **mech'-kō** メチ公 or **jogak'sei** 女学生

co-existence **kyōzon** 共存

coffee **kōhii** コーヒー

coffeehouse **kōhii-ten** コーヒー店

coffee cup **kōhii-jawan** コーヒー茶碗

coin **tama** 玉 or **kōka** 硬貨; (*brass or copper*)
  dōka 銅貨; (10 Yen) **jū-en-dama**; (5 Yen)
  go-en-dama 十(五)円玉

colander **mizu-koshi** 水こし   「冷い」

cold **samui** 寒い; (*to the touch*) **tsumetai**
(catches) cold **kaze o hikimas'** (*hiku, hiite*)
  風邪を引く

coleslaw **kyabetsu-sarada** キャベツ・サラダ

collapse **tsuburemas'** (*tsubureru, tsuburete*)
  つぶれる

collar (*of coat*) **eri** えり; (*of dog*) **kubi-wa** 首輪

collect (*collects them*) **atsumemas'** (*atsumeru,
  atsumete*) 集める; (*they collect*) **atsumarimas'** (*atsumaru, atsumatte*) 集まる

33

college **daigaku** 大学

collision **shōtotsu** 衝突

colloquial (language) **kōgo** 口語

colonel **taisa** 大佐

colony **shokumin-chi** 植民地

color **iro** 色

comb **kushi** くし (櫛)

comb (the hair) **kami o tokashimas'** (*tokasu, tokash'te*) 髪をとかす

combination **kumi-awase** 組合せ

combine **awasemas'** (*awaseru, awasete*) 合せる

come **kimas'** (*kuru, kite*) 来る

comet **hōki-boshi** ほうき星

comfortable **raku** (na) 楽 (な)

comic book **manga-bon** 漫画本

comics **manga** 漫画 「-ts'kete」に言い付ける

command ... **ni ii-ts'kemas'** (*-ts'keru,*

commander (*navy*) 中佐 **chūsa**

commerce **shōgyō** 商業

committee **iinkai** 委員会

common **futsū** (no) 普通 (の)

Communism **Kyōsan-shugi** 共産主義

community **shakai** 社会

commute **kayoimas'** (*kayou, kayotte*) 通う

commuter's ticket **teiki** (ken) 定期 (券)

companion *see* friend

company (*firm*) **kaisha** 会社 「比べる

compare **kurabemas'** (*kuraberu, kurabete*)

compass (*for directions*) **rashimban** 羅針盤;

34

(*for drafting*) **kompasu** コンパス

complaint **fuhei** 不平 *or* **kogoto** 小言

completely **zembu** 全部 *or* **minna** 皆

complicated **fukuzatsu (na)** 複雑 (な) *or* **komi-itta** 込み入った

compliment **o-seji** お世辞

compromise **dakyō** 妥協

comrade **dōshi** 同志

conceal *see* hide

concert **ongakkai** 音楽会

condition (*state*) **arisama** 有様 *or* **jōtai** 状態; (*stipulation*) **jōken** 条件

condom **sakku** サック

conductor (*train, etc.*) **shashō(san)** 車掌(さん)

conference **sōdan** 相談; (*formal*) **kaigi** 会議

confess **uchi-akemas'** (*-akeru, -akete*) 打ち明ける

confidence **shin-yō** 信用; (self-) **jishin** 自信

confidential *see* secret

Confucianism **Jukyō** 儒教

Confucius **Kōshi** 孔子

confused **komarimas'** (*komaru, komatte*) 困る

Congratulations! **Omedetō gozaimas'.** おめでとうございます

conjunction **setsuzoku-shi** 接続詞

(it) connects (with) ... **to renraku shimas'** (*suru, sh'te*) と連絡する 「関係

connection **renraku** 連絡; (*relevance*) **kankei**

conscience **ryōshin** 良心

conscientious **majime** (*na*) まじめ(な)

consent **shōchi shimas'** (*suru, sh'te*) 承知する

consequence *see* result 「考える

consider **kangaemas'** (*kangaeru, kangaete*)

considerable **sōtō** 相当 「やり

consideration (*being kind*) **omoiyari** おもい

consonant **shiin** *or* **shion** 子音

constantly *see* always

constipation **bempi** 便秘

construction (work) **kōji** 工事

consul **ryōji** 領事

consulate **ryōji-kan** 領事館

contact (*a person*) . . .**to renraku shimas'**
(*suru, sh'te*) と連絡する *or* . . .**ni aimas'**
(*au, atte*) に合う 「はいっている

contain . . .**ga haitte imas'** (*iru, ite*) が

contented (with) . . .**de manzoku shimas'**
(*suru, sh'te*) で満足する

contest **konkūru** コンクール

continent **tairiku** 大陸

continue (*it continues*) **tsuzukimas'** (*tsuzuku,*
tsuzuite) 続く; (*continues it*) **tsuzukemas'**
(*tsuzukeru, tsuzukete*) 続ける

contract **keiyaku** 契約

contradiction (*inconsistency*) **mujun** 矛盾

control (*supervise*) **tori-shimarimas'** (*-shima-*
ru, -shimatte) 取締る

convenient **benri** (*na*) 便利な

convent **shūdōin** 修道院

conversation (*ordinary*) **hanashi** 話; (*in language class, etc.*) **kaiwa** 会話

converter **henkanki** 変換器; (*AC-DC*) **henryū-ki** 変流機; (*transformer*) **hen-ats'ki** 変圧機

cook **kokku (san)** コック (さん); (*cooks it*) **ryōri shimas'** (*suru, sh'te*) 料理する

cool **suzushii** 涼しい

cooperation **kyōryoku** 協力

copper **aka-gane** or **dō** 銅　「*"it is," etc.*)

copula **shitei-shi** 指定詞 (*the word des'*)

copy (**ichi-**)**bu** (一) 部　「*utsush'te*)

copy (*makes a . . .*) **utsushimas'** (*utsusu,*

coral **sango** さんご

cord **himo** ひも

core **shin** 心

corkscrew **koruku-nuki** コルク抜き

corn **tō-morokoshi** とうもろこし 「**sumi** すみ

corner (*outside*) **kado** かど (角); (*inside*)

corporal **gochō** 伍長

corps **gundan** 軍団　　　　　　　「死人

corpse **shitai** 死体 or **shigai** 死骸 or **shinin**

correct **tadashii** 正しい

correspondence **tsūshin** 通信

corridor **rōka** 廊下

corrugated cardboard **dam-boru** 段ボール

cosmetics **keshō-hin** 化粧品

cost (*how much*) (**ikura**) **shimas'** (*suru,*

cotton **wata** わた (綿) 　 ⌊*sh'te*) (いくら) する

cough **seki o shimas'** (*suru, sh'te*) 咳をする

could *see* can

count **kazoemas'** (*kazoeru, kazoete*) 数える

counterclockwise **hidari-mawari** (ni) 左廻り
(に)

country (*nation*) **kuni** 国; (*farm*) **inaka** 田舎

county **gun** 郡

couple *see* two

course (*in school*) **kamoku** 科目

court (*law*) **saiban** 裁判

cousin **itoko** いとこ

cover (*lid*) **futa** ふた

cow **ushi** 牛

crab **kani** かに

crack (*wide*) **ware-me** 割れ目; (*fine*) **hibi** ひび

crackers **kurakkā** クラッカー *or* **bis'ketto**

cradle **yuri-kago** ゆりかご └ビスケット

crater **funka-kō** 噴火口

crazy **ki-chigai** (no) 気違い (の)

cream **kuriimu** クリーム

crime **tsumi** 罪 *or* **hanzai** 犯罪 「**fugu** 不具

cripple **katawa** 片輪 *or* **chimba** ちんば *or*

crock **tsubo** つぼ

crossing (*street intersection*) **kōsaten** 交叉点

crotch **mata** また

crow **karasu** からす

crowded **konde imas'** (*iru, ite*) こんでいる

cruel **zankoku** (na) 残酷 (な)

crush (*crushes it*) **tsubushimas'** (*tsubusu,
tsubush'te*) つぶす; (*it crushes*) **tsubure-**

mas' (*tsubureru, tsuburete*) つぶれる
crust **kawa** 皮
crutches **matsuba-zue** 松葉杖
cry **nakimas'** (*naku, naite*) 泣く
cuckoo **hototogisu** ほととぎす
cucumber **kyūri** きゅうり 「**bunka** 文化
culture (*refinement*) **kyōyō** 教養; (*civilization*)
cup **chawan** 茶碗; (*a . . . of*) **ip-pai** 一杯
cupboard **shokki-dana** 食器棚
cure **naoshimas'** (*naosu, naosh'te*) 直す
(gets) cured **naorimas'** (*naoru, naotte*) 直る
curios **kottō-hin** こっとう品
curious **monozuki** (**na**) 物好き (な)
curry **karē** カレー; (*with rice*) **karē-raisu**
　　カレー・ライス
curtains **kāten** カーテン *or* **mado-kake** 窓掛
cushion (*seat*) **zabuton** 座ぶとん
custom **shūkan** 習慣
customer **kyaku** 客; **o-kyaku san** お客さん
customs **kanzei** 関税
cut **kirimas'** (*kiru, kitte*) 切る
cute **kawaii** かわいい
cuttlefish (*squid*) **ika** いか
cypress **hinoki** ひのき

D

dairy **gyūnyū-ya** 牛乳屋 *or* **miruku-ten**
dam **damu** ダム　　　　　　└ミルク店

39

damascene **nie** にえ

damask **donsu** どんす

damp **shimeppoi** しめっぽい 「(をする)

dance **odori (o shimas'; suru, sh'te)** 踊り

dandruff **fuke** ふけ

danger **kiken** 危険

dangerous **abunai** 危い

dark **kurai** 暗い

date (*engagement*) **yakusoku** 約束

date (*a couple*) **abekku** アベック

date (*of month*) **hizuke** 日付け

daughter **musume (san)** むすめ(さん)

dawn **yoake** 夜明け

day **hi** 日; (*daytime*) **hiru (ma)** 昼(間)

day after tomorrow **asatte** あさって

day before yesterday **ototoi** おととい

D.C. (current) **chokuryū** 直流

dead **shinde imas' (iru, ite)** 死んでいる

deaf **tsumbo (no)** つんぼ(の)

debt **shakkin** 借金

deceive *see* cheat

December **Jūni-gatsu** 十二月

decide **kimemas' (kimeru, kimete)** 定める

decline (*refuse*) **kotowarimas' (kotowaru,**

deep **fukai** 深い ⎣**kotowatte**) ことわる

deer **sh'ka** 鹿 「負かす

defeat **makashimas' (makasu, makash'te)**

defend **mamorimas' (mamoru, mamotte)** 守る

degree (*extent*) **teido** 程度

40

(is) delayed **okuremas'** (*okureru, okurete*)
遅れる 「わざわざ
deliberately **waza to** わざと; **waza-waza**
delicious **oishii** おいしい *or* **umai** うまい
delightful **ureshii** うれしい 「届ける
deliver **todokemas'** (*todokeru, todokete*)
demand **motomemas'** (*motomeru, motomete*)
democracy **minshu-shugi** 民主主義 し求める
dentist **ha-isha** 歯医者
deny **uchi-keshimas'** (*-kesu, -kesh'te*) 打消す
deodorant **shūki-dome** 臭気止め
department store **depāto** デパート
depilatory **datsumō-zai** 脱毛剤
deposit **azukemas'** (*azukeru, azukete*) 預ける
depressed (*feeling*) **ki ga omoi** 気が重い
depression (*hard times*) **fukeiki** 不景気
describe ...(**no koto o**) **kuwashiku iimas'**
(*yū, yutte* or *itte*) (の事を) 詳しく言う
description **setsumei** 説明
desert **sabaku** さばく (砂漠) 「欲しい
desirable **nozomashii** 望ましい *or* **hoshii**
desire **hoshii** ほしい
desk **ts'kue** つくえ (机)
desperately **isshō-kemmei ni** 一生懸命に
dessert **dezāto** デザート 「こわす
destroy **kowashimas'** (*kowasu, kowash'te*)
detailed **kuwashii** 詳しい
detective **tantei** 探偵
detour **mawari-michi** 回り路 *or* **ukai** 迂回

41

or **tōmawari** 遠回り

device **kufū** 工夫; (*gadget*) **shikake** 仕掛け

devil **oni** 鬼

dew **tsuyu** つゆ (露)

diabetes **tōnyō-byō** 糖尿病

dialect **namari** 訛り *or* **hōgen** 方言

diapers **oshime** おしめ *or* **omutsu** おむつ

diarrhea **geri** 下痢

diary **nikki** 日記

dictation **kakitori** 書き取り

dictator **wam-man** ワンマン

dictionary **jibiki** 字引

did *see* do

die **shinimas'** (*shinu, shinde*) 死ぬ *or* **naku-narimas'** (*-naru, -natte*) なくなる

Diet (*parliament*) **Kokkai** 国会 *or* **Gikai** 議会

different **chigaimas'** (*chigau, chigatte*) 違う

difficult **muzukashii** むづかしい

dig **horimas'** (*horu, hotte*) 掘る

digest **konashimas'** (*konasu, konash'te*) こなす

dike **tsutsumi** 堤 *or* **dote** 土手

dimple **ekubo** えくぼ

diner (*on train*) **shokudō-sha** 食堂車

dining room **shokudō** 食堂

dinner **shokuji** 食事 *or* **gohan** 御飯

diplomat **gaikōkan** 外交官

direct **chokusetsu** 直接

direction **hō** 方 *or* **hōkō** 方向

directory (*telephone*) **denwa-chō** 電話帳

dirt **doro** 泥

dirty **kitanai** きたない 「がっかりする

disappointed **gakkari shimas'** (*suru, sh'te*)

discount **wari-biki** 割引

discourtesy **burei** 無礼 *or* **shitsurei** 失礼

discover **mi-tsukemas'** (*-tsukeru, -tsukete*)

disease **byōki** 病気 └見つける

disgraceful **hazukashii** はずかしい

disgusting **iya (na)** いや(な)

dish **sara** 皿

dishpan **sara-arai-oke** 皿洗い桶

disinfectant **shōdoku-zai** 消毒剤

dislike **...ga kirai des'** がきらいです

dispensary **yakkyoku** 薬局 「態度

disposition **seishitsu** 性質; (*attitude*) **taido**

dissipation **dōraku** 道楽

dissolve (*dissolves it*) **tokashimas'** (*tokasu,*
tokash'te) 溶かす; (*it dissolves*) **tokemas'**

distance **kyori** 距離 └(*tokeru, tokete*) 溶ける

distant *see* far

distinctly **hakkiri** はっきり

distress **nayami** 悩み

distribute **kubarimas'** (*kubaru, kubatte*) 配る

district **chihō** 地方 「をする

disturb **jama o shimas'** (*suru, sh'te*) じゃま

ditch **mizo** 溝

divide (*divides it*) **wakemas'** (*wakeru, wakete*)
分ける; (*it divides*) **wakaremas'** (*wakareru,*

divorce **rikon** 離婚 └*wakarete*) 分れる

43

do shimas' (*suru, sh'te*) する

dock **dokku** ドック

doctor (**o-**)**isha** (**san**) お医者 (さん)

Dr . . . . . . **sensei** 先生

dog **inu** 犬

doll **ningyō** 人形

Doll Festival **Hina-matsuri** 雛祭

dollar **doru** ドル

done (*ready*) **dekimash'ta** 出來ました *or*
  dekite imas' (*iru, ite*) 出來ている, (*finished*)
  . . . te shimaimash'ta (*shimatta, shimatte*)
  . . . てしまった

(half-)done (*medium*) **han-yake no** 半燒けの

(under) done (*rare*) **nama-yake no** 生燒けの

(well-)done **yoku yaketa** よく燒けた

donkey **roba** ろば

Don't! **Dame des'!** だめです

door **to** 戸

dope **mayaku** 麻薬

dormitory **kishuk'sha** 寄宿舎

dot **ten** 点

double **bai** (**no**) 倍 (の)

double-cross **ura-giri** 裏切

doubt **utagaimas'** (*utagau, utagatte*) 疑う

douche **chūsui-ki** 注水器

dough **neri-ko** 練粉 *or* **nama-pan** 生パン

dove **hato** はと

down **shita e** 下へ

(gets) down **orimas'** (*oriru, orite*) 下りる

44

(one) dozen (**ichi-**)**dāsu** (1) ダース or **jū ni** 十二

drag **hipparimas'** (*hipparu, hippatte*) 引っぱる

dragon **ryū** 竜

drain (*kitchen*) **gesui** 下水

dramamine **doramamin** ドラマミン

drapes **kāten** カーテン 　　　　　「描く

draw (a picture) **egakimas'** (*egaku, egaite*)

drawer (*of desk, etc.*) **hiki-dashi** 引出し

drawers (*underwear*) **zubon-sh'ta** ズボン下

dreadful **osoroshii** 恐ろしい

dream **yume** (**o mimas'**; *miru, mite*) 夢(を見る)

dress **kimono** (**o kimas'**; *kiru, kite*) 着物
　(を着る) 　　　　　　　「**mēka** ドレス・メーカ

dressmaker **yōsai(-shi)** 洋裁師 or **doresu-**

drink **nomimas'** (*nomu, nonde*) 飲む

drinking water **nomi-mizu** 飲水 　「運転する

drive (a car) **unten shimas'** (*suru, sh'te*)

drive-in **nori-komi** 乗り込み

driver **unten-shu** 運転手

driveway **shadō** 車道

drop **otoshimas'** (*otosu, otosh'te*) 落す

drown **obore-jini shimas'** (*suru, sh'te*) 溺れ

drug **k'suri** 薬 　　　　　　　　　└死にする

drugstore **k'suri-ya** 薬屋 　　　　　　「鼓

drum **taiko** 太鼓; (*hourglass-shaped*) **tsuzumi**

(gets) drunk **yopparaimas'** (*yopparau,*
　yopparatte) よっぱらう

dry (*it dries*) **kawakimas'** (*kawaku, kawaite*)
　乾く; (*dries it*) **kawakashimas'** (*kawa-*

45

kasu, kawakash'te) 乾かす

dry cleaning **dorai-kuriiningu** ドライ・クリー「ニング

duck (*wild*) **kamo** 鴨; (*tame*) **ahiru** あひる

due to *see* because; *see* supposed to

dull **nibui** 鈍い; (*uninteresting*) **taikutsu (na)** 退屈（な）

dumpling (*large meat-stuffed*) **manjū** まんじゅう; (*small meat-stuffed*) **gyōza** ぎょうざ

dung **k'so** 糞

during (*. . . no*) **aida** （の）間

dust (*on ground*) **chiri** ちり; (*in air*) **hokori** ほこり; (*in house*) **gomi** ごみ

dust pan **chiri tori** チリ取り

Dutch **Oranda(-jin)** オランダ（人）

(going) Dutch **wari-kan** 割勘

duty **gimu** 義務 *or* **hombun** 本分

(is on) duty **tōban (des')** 当番（です）

duty (*import*) **yunyūzei** 輸入税; *see also* customs

dwarf trees **bonsai** 盆栽

dwindle **herimas'** (*heru, hette*) 減る *or* **chiisaku narimas'** (*naru, natte*) 小さくなる

dye **somemas'** (*someru, somete*) 染める

E

each **. . . zutsu** ずつ

eagerly **nesshin ni** 熱心に

eagle **washi** わし

ear **mimi** 耳

46

early hayai (hayaku) 早い（早く）

earn kasegimas' (*kasegu, kaseide*) かせぐ

earnest majime (na) まじめ（な）

earth tsuchi 土

earthenware doki 土器

earthquake jishin 地震

east higashi 東

easy yasashii やさしい

eat tabemas' (*taberu, tabete*) 食べる

echo hibiki 響き

economics keizai 経済

economize ken-yaku shimas' (*suru, sh'te*) 「検約する

edge fuchi ふち; (*of knife*) **ha** 刃

education kyōiku 教育

eel unagi うなぎ　　　　　「**kiki-me** 利目

effect (*result*) **kekka** 結果; (*effectiveness*)

(is) effective kikimas' (*kiku, kiite*) 利く

efficiency nōritsu 能率

effort hone-ori 骨折り

egg tamago 卵

eight hachi 八 **or yattsu** 八つ

eighteen jū hachi 十八

eighty hachi-jū 八十

either one dochira de mo どちらでも

elastic (*material*) **gomu** ゴム

elbow hiji 肘

elect erabimas' (*erabu, erande*) 選ぶ

election senkyo 選挙

electricity denki 電気

elegant **fūryū (na)** 風流(な)

elephant **zō** 象

elevator **erebētā** エレベーター

eleven **jū ichi** 十一

else **hoka ni** 外に 「困る

embarrassed **komarimas'** (*komaru, komatte*)

embassy **taishikan** 大使館 「**sama** 天皇様

Emperor **Tennō-heika** 天皇階下 *or* **Tennō-**

employ **yatoimas'** (*yatou, yatotte*) 雇う

(is) employed **tsutomete imas'** (*iru, ite*)
勤めている 「皇后様

Empress **Kōgō-heika** 皇后階下 *or* **Kōgō-sama**

empty **kara (no)** から(の) *or* **karappo (no)**
からっぽ(の) 「*owatte*) 終る

end **owari** 終り; (*it ends*) **owarimas'** (*owaru,*
(*goes to the*) end (*of a road, etc.*) **ts'ki-**
atarimas' (*-ataru, -atatte*) 突き当る

enema **kanchō** 灌腸

enemy **teki** 敵

energy **ikioi** 勢

engaged (*to be married*) **kon-yaku sh'te**
imas' (*iru, ite*) 婚約している

engagement (*date*) **yak'soku** 約束

engine **kikan** 機関

engineer **gishi** 技師

England **Eikoku** 英国

English **Eigo** 英語

Englishman **Eikoku-jin** 英国人 「楽しむ

enjoy **tanoshimimas'** (*tanoshimu, tanoshinde*)

48

enough **jūbun** (na) 充分 (な)

ensign **shōi** 少尉

enter (... **ni** or ... **no naka ni**) **hairimas'**
(*hairu, haitte*) (の中に) 入る 「馳走する

entertain **gochisō shimas'** (*suru, sh'te*) 御

enthusiastic **nesshin** (na) 熱心 (な)

entire **zentai no** 全体の

entrance **iri-guchi** 入口

envelope **fūtō** 封筒 「うらやむ

envy **urayamimas'** (*urayamu, urayande*)

equal **hitoshii** 等しい

equipment **sōchi** 装置 or **setsubi** 設備

erase **keshimas'** (*kesu, kesh'te*) 消す

eraser (*pencil*) **keshi-gomu** 消ゴム; (*blackboard*) **kokuban-fuki** 黒板ふき

erect **tatemas'** (*tateru, tatete*) 建てる

erotic **iroppoi** 色っぽい or **kōshoku** 好色

errand **ts'kai** 使い

errand boy **o-ts'kai san** お使いさん

error **machigai** 間違い

escape **nigemas'** (*nigeru, nigete*) 逃げる

especially **tokubetsu ni** 特別に or **koto ni**

essential **hitsuyō** (na) 必要 (な) 　└殊に

establish **tatemas'** (*tateru, tatete*) 建てる

etiquette **reigi** 礼儀

Europe **Yōroppa** ヨーロッパ

evaporated milk **nōshuku gyūnyū** 濃縮牛乳
or **kona-miruku** 粉ミルク

even... ...**de mo**

evening **ban** 晩 *or* **yūgata** 夕方

ever (*once*) **itsu ka** いつか; (*always*) **itsu mo** いつも

every... **dono ... de mo** どのでも いいつも

everybody **minna** 皆 *or* **dare de mo** 誰でも

everything **minna** 皆 *or* **nan de mo** 何でも

everywhere **doko ni mo** どこにも *or* **doko de mo** どこでも

evil *see* bad

exact (*detailed*) **kuwashii** 詳しい; (*correct*) **seikaku (na)** 正確 (な)

exactly **chōdo** 丁度 *or* **mattaku** 全く

examination **sh'ken** 試験

example **rei** 例

excellent **sugureta** すぐれた

except (for)... **... no hoka** の外

exception **reigai** 例外

excessive **yokei (na)** 余計 (な)

exchange **tori-kaemas'** (*-kaeru, -kaete*) 取換える *or* **kōkan shimas'** (*suru, sh'te*) 交換する

(gets) excited **ki ga tachimas'** (*tatsu, tatte*) 気が立つ

excursion **ensoku** 遠足 *or* **yūran** 遊覧

Excuse me. **Sumimasen.** すみません *or* **Gomen nasai.** ごめんなさい

exercise (*physical*) **taisō** 体操

existence **sonzai** 存在

exit **deguchi** 出口

expect (*await*) **matte imas'** (*iru, ite*) 待っている

expects to (do) **...(suru) tsumori des'** (する) つもりです

50

expensive **(ne ga) takai** (値が) 高い

experience **keiken** 経験 「達者 (な)

expert **jōzu (na)** 上手 (な) *or* **tassha (na)**

explain **setsumei shimas'** *(suru, sh'te)* 説明する

export **yushutsu shimas'** *(suru, sh'te)* 輸出する

extend **nobashimas'** *(nobasu, nobash'te)* 伸ばす

extra **yobun ni** 余分に *or* **betsu (na)** 別 (な)

extravagance **zeitaku** 贅沢

extremely **hijō ni** 非常に *or* **kiwamete** 極めて
or **hanahada** はなはだ *or* **shigoku** 至極

eye **me** 目 「*or* **mono-sugoku** ものすごく

eyebrow **mayuge** まゆげ

F

fabric **orimono** 織物

face **kao** 顔 「**wa** 実は

fact **jijitsu** 事実 *or* **koto** 事: (*in . . .*) **jitsu**

factory **kōba** 工場

fade **samemas'** *(sameru, samete)* 褪める

fail *(in school, etc.)* **rakudai shimas'** *(suru,
sh'te)* 落第する 「気を失う

faint **ki o ushinaimas'** *(ushinau, ushinatte)*

fair *(just)* **kōhei (na)** 公平 (な)

fair *(market)* **ichi** 市

fake **nisemono** にせもの

fall **ochimas'** *(ochiru, och'te)* 落ちる *or* **ok-
kochimas'** *(okkochiru, okkoch'te)*

false **uso** 嘘

51

false teeth **ire-ba** 入歯

familiar **shitashii** 親しい

family **uchi** 家 *or* **kazoku** 家族

famous **yūmei na** 有名な *or* **na-dakai** 名高い

fan (*folding*) **sensu** 扇子; (*flat*) **uchiwa** うちわ

far **tōi** 遠い ⌊(*electric*) **sempūki** 扇風機

farmer **hyak'shō** 百姓

fast **hayaku, hayai** 速く(い)

fat (*gets fat*) **f'torimas'** (*f'toru, f'totte*) 肥る、

  (*is fat*) **f'totte imas'** (*iru, ite*) 肥っています

fate **un** 運

father **otōsan** お父さん *or* **chichi(-oya)** 父(親)

Father ... (*Reverend*) ... **Shimpu san** 神

  父さん   「**desh'ta.** (私が)悪いでした

(It was my) fault. (**Watashi ga**) **warui**

favor **shinsetsu** 親切

favorite **ichiban s'ki** (**na**) 一番好き(な)

fear **osoremas'** (*osoreru, osorete*) 恐れる

feather **hane** 羽

February **Ni-gatsu** 二月

feeble **yowai** 弱い   「食べさせる

feed **tabesasemas'** (*tabesaseru, tabesasete*)

feel (*by touch*) **sawarimas'** (*sawaru, sawatte*)

  触る; (*by emotion*) **kanjimas'** (*kanjiru*,

feeling **kimochi** 気持   ⌊*kanjite*) 感じる

(it) feels (good) **kimochi ga ii** 気持がいい

fellow **hito** 人 *or* **mono** 者

female **onna** 女

fence **kakine** 垣根

52

ferryboat **watashi-bune** 渡し舟

festival **matsuri** 祭

feudal (*system*) **hōken(-seido)** 封建制度

fever **netsu** 熱

few **s'koshi** (no) 少し(の); **s'kunai** 少い

fickle **uwaki** (na) 浮気(な)

field (*dry*) **hatake** 畑; (*rice*) **ta** 田 or **tambo**

fierce **hageshii** 烈しい or **sugoi** すごい

fifteen **jū go** 十五

fifty **go-jū** 五十

fight **tatakaimas'** (*tatakau, tatakatte*) 戦う

figure *see* count; *see* think; *see* body

file (*like nail file*) **yasuri** やすり

fill **ippai ni shimas'** (*suru, sh'te*) 一杯にする

film **fuirumu** フィルム

filthy *see* dirty

finance **zaisei** 財政

find **mits'kemas'** (*mits'keru, mits'kete*) 見付ける

fine *see* good

finger **yubi** 指

finish *see* end; (*finishes it*) **sumashimas'**
 (*sumasu, sumash'te*) すます

fire **hi** 火; (*accidental*) **kaji** 火事

fire (*dismiss, discharge*) (...ni) **hima o dashimas'** (*dasu, dash'te*) 暇を出す

fire hydrant **shōbōsen** 消防栓

fireman **shōbōfu** 消防夫

fireworks **hana-bi** 花火

first **hajime no** 初めの or **saisho no** 最初の;

(*class in trains, etc.*) **ittō** 一等; (*of hotels,*

fish **sakana** 魚 ⌊*etc.*) **ichi-ryū (no)** 一流(の)

fisherman **gyofu** 漁夫

fishing (*as sport*) **tsuri** 釣

fist **kobushi** こぶし

five **go** 五 *or* **itsutsu** 五つ

fix (*repair*) **naoshimas'** (*naosu, naosh'te*) 直す

flag **hata** 旗

flashlight **kaichū-dentō** 懐中電灯

flat **taira (na)** 平(な)

flatulence **onara** おなら

flea **nomi** のみ

flesh **nikutai** 肉体

float **ukabimas'** (*ukabu, ukande*) 浮ぶ

flood **ōmizu** 大水

floor **yuka** 床

florist **hana-ya** 花屋

flour **ko** 粉; (*wheat*) **meriken-ko** メリケン粉

flow **nagaremas'** (*nagareru, nagarete*) 流れる

flower **hana** 花 ⌈ing) **ikebana** 生花

flower arrangement **o-hana** お花 *or* (arrang-

flowerpot **ueki-bachi** 植木鉢

flower viewing **hana-mi** 花見

fly (*insect*) **hae** はえ

fly (*moves in air*) **tobimas'** (*tobu, tonde*) 飛ぶ

foam *see* bubble

focus **pinto** ピント

fog **kiri** 霧 ⌈折りたたむ

fold up **ori-tatamimas'** (*-tatamu, -tatande*)

folks *see* people; *see* parents; *see* family

follow . . . no ato o ts'kemas' (*ts'keru, ts'kete*)

following **tsugi (no)** 次 (の)　└の後を附ける

fond of *see* like

food **tabemono** 食べ物 *or* **gohan** 御飯; (A-merican) **yōshoku** 洋食; (Japanese) **washo-**

fool **baka** ばか　└**ku** 和食

foolish **baka-rashii** ばからしい *or* **baka (na)**

foot **ashi** 足　　　　　└ばか (な)

footstool **ashi-dai** 足台

for (no) **tame (ni)** (の) ため (に)

forbid **kinjimas'** (*kinjiru, kinjite*) 禁じる

force (to do) **muri ni** (*or* **shiite**) **sasemas'** (*saseru, sasete*) 無理に (強いて) させる

foreign **gaikoku (no)** 外国 (の)

foreigner **gaijin** 外人

forest **hayashi** 林 *or* **mori** 森

forever *see* always　　　　　└忘れる

forget **wasuremas'** (*wasureru, wasurete*)

forgive **yurushimas'** (*yurusu, yurush'te*) 許す

fork **fōku** フォーク *or* **hōku** ホーク

form **katachi** 形

former **mae no** 前の

fortune **zaisan** 財産; (*luck*) **un** 運

fortunetelling **uranai** 占い

forty **yon-jū** *or* **shi-jū** 四十

forward **mae ni** 前に

foul *see* dirty

found *see* find; *see* establish

55

fountain pen **mannenhitsu** 万年筆

four **yon** *or* **shi** 四 *or* **yottsu** 四つ

four people **yo-nin** 四人

four o'clock **yo-ji** 四時

fourteen **jū yon** *or* **jū shi** 十四

fox **kitsune** 狐

fragile **koware-yasui** こわれやすい

frame **waku** 枠

France **Furansu** フランス

free (*gratis*) **tada (no)** 只の; (*as part of the service*) **sābisu** サービス

freely **jiyū ni** 自由に

freeze (*it freezes*) **kōrimas'** (*kōru, kōtte*) 凍る; (*freezes it*) **kōrasemas'** (*kōraseru, kōrasete*) 凍らせる

French (language) **Furansu-go** フランス語

frequently *see* often

fresh **atarashii** 新しい

Friday **kin-yōbi** 金曜日

friend **tomodachi** 友達

frog **kaeru** 蛙

from . . . **. . . kara** から

front **mae** 前

frost **shimo** 霜

fruit **kudamono** 果物

fry **agemas'** (*ageru, agete*) 揚げる

frying pan **age-nabe** あげなべ

Fuji-yama **Fuji(-san)** 富士(山)

full **ippai (no)** 一杯(の)

fun omoshiroi koto おもしろい事
(This is) fun! Omoshiroi des' ne! おもしろいですね
funeral o-sōsh'ki お葬式
funnel rōto 漏斗
funny okashii おかしい or kokkei (na) こっけい(な) or yukai (na) 愉快(な)
fur ke-gawa 毛皮
furnace kamado かまど
furnish (provide) sonaemas' (sonaeru, sonaete) 備える
furniture kagu 家具
further hoka (ni) 外(に)
fuss sawagi 騒ぎ
futile muda むだ
future shōrai 将來

G

gain see get
gambling tobaku とばく or bakuchi ばくち
game asobi 遊び or gēmu ゲーム
gap s'kima 隙間
garbage gomi ごみ
garbage man gomi-ya ごみ屋
garden niwa 庭
gardener ueki-ya 植木屋
garlic ninniku にんにく
garter gātā ガーター
gas gasu ガス; (gasoline) gasorin ガソリン

gas(oline) station **gasorin s'tando** ガソリン・スタンド

gasp **aegimas'** (*aegu, aeide*) 喘ぐ

gate **mon** 門

gather (*they gather*) **atsumarimas'** (*atsumaru, atsumatte*) 集まる; (*gathers them*) **atsumemas'** (*atsumeru, atsumete*) 集める

gaudy **hade** (na) はで(な)

gay **akarui** 明るい *or* **yukai** (na) 愉快(な)

general (*over-all*) **ippan** (no) 一般(の)

general (*army*) **taishō** 大将

generous **kandai** (na) 寛大な

gentle **yasashii** やさしい

gentleman **shinshi** 紳士 「(no) 真(の)

genuine **hommono** (no) 本物(の) *or* **makoto**

geography **chiri** 地理

geology **chishitsu** 地質

germ **baikin** ばい菌

German (language) **Doitsu-go** ドイツ語

Germany **Doitsu** ドイツ

gesture **temane** 手まね

get (*receive*) **moraimas'** (*morau, moratte*) 貰う; see also go, buy, take, become, etc.

get off (*get down*) **orimas'** (*oriru, orite*) 下りる

get up (*arise*) **okimas'** (*okiru, okite*) 起きる

ghost **obake** お化け *or* **bakemono** 化物

gift **okurimono** 贈り物

ginger **shōga** しょうが

girdle **koshi-obi** 腰帯

girl **musume** (san) むすめ(さん)

gist **yōshi** 要旨 or **yōten** 要点

give 1. (he to you, you to me) **kuremas'** (kureru, kurete) 呉れる or **kudasaimas'** (kudasaru, kudasatte) 下さる 2. (I to you, you to him, he to him) **agemas'** (ageru, agete) 上げる or **yarimas'** (yaru, yatte) やる

gladly **yorokonde** 喜んで

glass (the substance) **garasu** ガラス; (the container) **koppu** コップ, **gurasu** グラス, **gurasu-koppu** グラス・コップ

glasses **megane** めがね

gloomy **uttōshii** うっとうしい

glove **tebukuro** 手袋

glow **hikarimas'** (hikaru, hikatte) 光る

glue **nikawa** にかわ

glutinous rice **mochi-gome** もち米

go **ikimas'** (iku, itte) 行く

goat **yagi** やぎ

God **Kami(-sama)** 神(様)

godown (storeroom) **kura** 倉

gold **kin** 金

gonorrhea **rimbyō** 痳病

good **ii** いい or **yoi** よい

Good-bye. **Sayōnara** さようなら

goods **shinamono** 品物

goose **gachō** がちょう

gorgeous **rippa** (na) 立派(な)

gossip **uwasa** うわさ

government **seifu** 政府

governor **chiji** 知事

gradually **dandan** だんだん or **s'koshi zutsu**

graduate **sotsugyō shimas'** (*suru, sh'te*) 卒業する

grain (*one*) **tsubu** つぶ; (*cereal*) **kokumotsu**

grammar **bumpō** 文法

grand **subarashii** 素晴しい or **erai** えらい

grandchild **mago** 孫

grandfather **ojii-san** おじいさん

grandmother **obaa-san** おばあさん

grapes **budō** ぶどう

grass **k'sa** 草

(I am) grateful. **Arigataku zonjimas'.** (*zonjiru, zonjite*) ありがたく存じます

grave (*tomb*) **haka** 墓

gray **hai-iro (no)** 灰色 (の) or **nezumi-iro**

grease **abura** あぶら

great *see* big; *see* good

greedy **kui-shimbō (na)** 食いしん坊 (な)

green **midori (no)** 緑 (の)

greens **aomono** 青物

greeting **aisatsu** 挨拶

grill **aburimas'** (*aburu, abutte*) あぶる

groan **umekimas'** (*umeku, umeite*) うめく

grocery store **shokuryōhin-ten** 食料品店

ground **jimen** 地面

group (*class*) **kumi** 組; (*crowd, flock*) **mure** 群

grow **ōkiku narimas'** (*naru, natte*) 大きくなる

60

gruel (*rice*) **o-kayu** おかゆ

guard **mamorimas'** (*mamoru, mamotte*) 守る

guess **atemas'** (*ateru, atete*) 当てる; *see also* understand

guest **kyaku** 客, **o-kyaku san** お客さん

guide (*person*) **annai-sha** 案内者; (*book*) **annai-sho** 案内書; (*guides him*) **annai shimas'** (*suru, sh'te*) 案内する

guilt **tsumi** 罪

gulf **wan** 湾

gull **kamome** かもめ

gum (*chewing*) **gamu** ガム

gun **jū** 銃 *or* **teppō** 鉄砲

gutter **dobu** どぶ

H

habit **shūkan** 習慣; (*bad one*) **kuse** 癖

hail **arare** (*ga furimas; furu, futte*) あられ (が降る)

hair (*on head*) **kami** 髪; (*elsewhere*) **ke** 毛

hairdresser *see* beauty parlor

hair oil **kami-abura** 髪油; (*stick pomade*) **chikku** チック

half **hambun** 半分

hall **kaikan** 会館; (*entrance*) **genkan** 玄関

halt *see* stop

ham **hamu** ハム

hammer **kanazuchi** かなづち

hand **te** 手　　　「*(watasu, watash'te)* 渡す

hand (something to a person) **watashimas'**

handkerchief **hankechi** ハンケチ

handle **totte** とって (把手)

handy *see* convenient

hangs (*it hangs*) **kakarimas'** *(kakaru, kakatte)* 掛る; (*hangs it*) **kakemas'** *(kakeru, kakete)* 掛ける

happen **okorimas'** *(okoru, okotte)* 起る

happiness **kōf'ku** 幸福

happy **ureshii** うれしい

hard **katai** 堅い　　　「(ない)

hardly **hotondo** + NEGATIVE **(nai)** ほとんど

hardware **kanagu** 金具

harm **gai** 害

harp (*Japanese*) **koto** 琴

hash **hayashi** 林

hasten *see* hurry

hat **bōshi** 帽子

hatchet **nata** 鉈 *or* **te-ono** 手斧

hate **iya des'** いやです; **kirai des'** きらいです

have (*...ga*) **arimas'** *(aru, atte)* ある *or* **motte imas'** *(iru, ite)* 持っている

hawk **taka** たか

hay **magusa** まぐさ

he **kare** 彼 *or* **ano hito** あの人

head **atama** 頭

headquarters **hombu** 本部 *or* **shireibu** 司令部

health **kenkō** 健康

healthy **genki** (na) 元気(な) **jōbu** (na) 丈夫(な)

hear **kikimas'** (*kiku, kiite*) 聞く ⌈**kokoro** 心

heart **shinzō** 心臓; (*as seat of emotions*)

heat **atsu-sa** 暑(熱)さ; (*heats it*) **ats'ku shimas'** (*suru, sh'te*) 熱くする; (*it heats up*) **ats'ku narimas'** (*naru, natte*) 熱くなる

heater **hiitā** ヒーター *or* **kanetsu-ki** 加熱器

heating (*of room, etc.*) **dambō** 暖房

heaven **tengoku** 天国

heavy **omoi** 重い

hedge **ikegaki** 生垣

heel **kakato** かかと

hell **jigoku** 地獄

Hello. (*on phone*) **Moshi moshi.** (*on street, in morning*) **Ohayō gozaimas'.** (*daytime*) **Konnichi wa.** (*evening*) **Komban wa.**

help (*assist*) **tetsudaimas'** (*tetsudau, tetsudatte*) 手伝う; (*save*) **tas'kemas'** (*tas'keru, tas'kete*) ⌊助ける

hemorrhoids **ji** 痔

her *see* she

here **koko** ここ ⌈ちょする

hesitate **chūcho shimas'** (*suru, sh'te*) ちゅう

hey! **oi!** おい! *or* **moshi-moshi!** もしもし!

hi! *see* hello; *see* hey

hiccup **shakkuri** しゃっくり

hide (*hides it*) **kakushimas'** (*kakusu, kakush'te*) 隠す; (*it hides*) **kakuremas'** (*kaku-*

high **takai** 高い ⌊*reru, kakurete*) 隠れる

highway **kokudō** 国道 *or* **kōdō** 公道

hill (*road*) saka 坂; (*small mountain*) oka 丘

him *see* he

hip koshi 腰 *or* shiri 尻

hire yatoimas' (*yatou, yatotte*) 雇う

history rekishi 歴史

hit buts'kemas' (*buts'keru, buts'kete*) ぶつける
 or uchimas' (*utsu, utte*) 打つ

hold (te ni) mochimas' (*motsu, motte*) (手に)持つ

hole ana 穴

holiday yasumi 休み; (*official*) saijitsu 祭日

home uchi 家

homesick (uchi ga) natsukashii (家が) なつかしい

honest shōjiki (na) 正直 (な)

honey mitsu 蜜 *or* hachi-mitsu はち蜜

honorific (*word*) keigo 敬語

hook kagi 鉤

hope nozomimas' (*nozomu, nozonde*) 望む

horn (*of animal*) tsuno 角

horrible osoroshii おそろしい

horse uma 馬

horseradish wasabi わさび

hospital byōin 病院

hot atsui 暑(熱)い

hot water o-yu お湯

hot-water bottle yu-tampo 湯たんぽ

hotel hoteru ホテル

hour jikan 時間

house uchi 家

housewife shufu 主婦

how **dō** どう

however **keredomo** けれども *or* **sh'kashi**

human being **ningen** 人間

humble (*modest*) **kenson shimas'** (*suru, sh'te*)

humid (*in summer*) **mushi-atsui** 蒸し暑い; (*in winter*) **shimeppoi** 湿っぽい

hundred **hyaku** 百

hungry **onaka ga s'kimash'ta** お腹が空き ました

hunt **kari** *or* **ryō o shimas'** (*suru, sh'te*) 狩をする

hurray! **banzai!** 万歳

hurricane **bōfū** 暴風

hurry **isogimas'** (*isogu, isoide*) 急ぐ

hurt **itai des'** 痛いです

husband **danna-san** だんなさん *or* **shujin** 主人

hygiene **eisei** 衛生

I

I **watashi** 私

ice **kōri** 氷

ice cream **ais'-kuriimu** アイスクリーム

idea **kangae** 考

if **moshi** もし

ill *see* sick; *see* bad

illegal **fuhō** (**na**) 不法 (な)

imagine *see* think

imitate **... no mane o shimas'** (*suru, sh'te*) の真似をする

imitation (*man-made*) **... jinzō ...** 人造

immediately **sugu** すぐ

65

impatient **ki ga mijikai** 気が短い

Imperial . . . **Teikoku** . . . 帝国

impolite **burei (na)** 無礼(な)

import **yunyū shimas'** (*suru, sh'te*) 輸入する

important **jūyō (na)** 重要 (な) *or* **taisetsu (na)** 大切(な)

impossible **dekinai** 出来ない *or* **fukanō(na)**

impression **inshō** 印象

improve (*it improves*) **naorimas'** (*naoru, na-otte*) 直る *or* **yoku narimas'** (*naru, natte*) よくなる; (*improves it*) **naoshimas'** (*naosu, naosh'te*) 直す *or* **yoku shimas'** (*suru, sh'te*) よくする

in . . . **ni** に *or* . . . **no naka ni** の中に

incense **kō** 香

inch (*Japanese*) **sun** 寸; (*American*) **inchi**

income **shotoku** 所得 *or* **shūnyū** 収入

income tax **shotoku-zei** 所得税

inconvenient **fuben (na)** 不便(な)

increase **mashimas'** (*masu, mash'te*) 増す

indecent **waisetsu(na)** わいせつ(な)

indeed **honto ni** ほんとに

independence **dokuritsu** 独立

India **Indo** インド

indigestion **fushōka** 不消化

indirect **kansetsu (na)** 間接(な)

individually **betsu-betsu ni** 別々に

indoors **uchi (no naka) ni** *or* **de** 家 (の中) に *or* で

industry **kōgyō** 工業 or **sangyō** 産業

influence **eikyō** 影響

inform **shirasemas'** (*shiraseru, shirasete*)

infrequently **tama ni** たまに or **mare ni** 稀に

injection **chūsha** 注射

injury **kega** 怪我

ink **inki** インキ

Inland Sea **Seto-Naikai** 瀬戸内海

inn (*Japanese hotel*) **ryokan** 旅館

inquire *see* ask

insane **ki-chigai** 気違い

insect **mushi** 虫

inside **naka ni** 中に

instead (**sono**) **kawari ni** (その)代りに

instruct *see* teach

instructor **kyōshi** 教師 or **sensei** 先生

insult **bujoku** 侮辱

insurance **hoken** 保険

intelligent **rikō** (na) 利口(な)

intend to (do) ... (**suru**) **tsumori des'** (する)

interest (*on mony*) **rishi** 利子

interest (*pleasure*) **kyōmi** 興味

interesting **omoshiroi** おもしろい

interfere **jama ni narimas'** (*naru, natte*)
じゃまになる or **jama o shimas'** (*suru,
sh'te*) じゃまをする

international **kok'sai no** 国際の

interpreter **tsūyaku** 通訳

interview **menkai** 面会

intestines **harawata** 腸

intimate **shitashii** したしい

intoxicated *see* drunk

introduce **shōkai shimas'** (*suru, sh'te*) 紹介する

invention **hatsumei** 発明 　　　　　「調べる

investigate **shirabemas'** (*shiraberu, shirabete*)

invite **yobimas'** (*yobu, yonde*) 呼ぶ *or* ma-
nekimas' (*maneku, maneite*) 招く *or* **shōtai shimas'** (*suru, sh'te*) 招待する

iodine **yōdo** ヨウド

Ireland **Airurando** アイルランド

iron (*the metal*) **tetsu** 鉄; (*clothes iron*) **airon**
アイロン; (*irons clothes*) **kimono ni airon
o kakemas'** (*kakeru, kakete*) 着物にアイロン
をかける

irregular **fukisoku (na)** 不規則 (な)

is (am, are, be) 1. (*it is*) ...**des'** (*da or na
or no, de*) だ 2. (*there is; it is in a place*)
arimas' (*aru, atte*) ある 3. (*he is in a place*)
imas' (*iru, ite*) 居る *or* **orimas'** (*oru, otte*)
居る 4. (*is doing*) ...**-te imas'** (*iru, ite*)
or ...**-te orimas'** (*oru, otte*) ...て居る

island **shima** 島

isn't (aren't) 1. (*it isn't*) ...**ja arimasen**
(*ja nai, ja nakute*) じゃない 2. (*there isn't*)
arimasen (*nai, nakute*) 無い

it *usually omitted in Japanese; or* **sore** それ

Italy **Itariya** イタリヤ

itch(y) **kaii** (*or* **kayui**) かゆい

68

ivory **zōge** 象牙

J

jade **kōgyoku** 硬玉
jail **rōgoku** 牢獄
jam *(to eat)* **jamu** ジャム
janitor **kozukai** 小使
January **Ichi-gatsu** 一月 *or* **Shōgatsu** 正月
Japan **Nihon** *or* **Nippon** 日本
Japanese (language) **Nihon-go** 日本語
Japanese *(person)* **Nihon-jin** 日本人
Japanese *(of Japan)* **Nihon no** 日本の
jar *(with large mouth)* **kame** かめ; *(with small
mouth)* **tsubo** 壺
jaundice **ōdan** 黄疸
jaw **ago** あご
jealous **yakimochi o yakimas'** *(yaku, yaite* 「焼餅を焼く
jelly **zeri** ゼリ *or* **jeri** ジェリ
jellyfish **kurage** くらげ
Jew **Yudaya-jin** ユダヤ人
jewel **hōseki** 宝石
job **shigoto** 仕事
join *(joins them together)* **awasemas'** *(awaseru, awasete)* 合せる; *(enters)* **...ni hairimas'** *(hairu, haitte)* に入る
joke **jōdan** じょうだん（冗談）
journey *see* trip
judge **saiban-kan** 裁判官
juice **jūsu** ジュース; **shiru** 汁

July **Shichi-gatsu** 七月
jump **tobimas'** (*tobu, tonde*) 跳ぶ
June **Roku-gatsu** 六月
just (*exact*) **chōdo** ちょうど(丁度)

K

keep **tamochimas'** (*tamotsu, tamotte*) 保つ
ketchup **kechappu** ケチャップ
kettle **kama** 釜
key **kagi** 鍵
kick **kerimas'** (*keru, kette*) 蹴る
kidneys **jinzō** 腎臓
kill **koroshimas'** (*korosu, korosh'te*) 殺す
kind (*nice*) **shinsetsu** (*na*) 親切(な)
kind (*variety*) **shurui** 種類
kindergarten **yōchien** 幼稚園
king **ō-sama** 王様 「*suru, sh'te*」(する)
kiss **kisu** キス *or* **seppun** 接吻 (**shimas'**;
kitchen **daidokoro** 台所
kite **tako** たこ
knee **hiza** 膝
knife **naifu** ナイフ; (*big*) **hōchō** 庖丁
knit **amimas'** (*amu, ande*) 編む
knitted goods **meriyasu** メリヤス
knock (on door) (**to o**) **tatakimas'** (*tataku, tataite*) (戸を) たたく
knot **musubi(-me)** 結び(目)
know **shitte imas'** (*iru, ite*) 知っている

70

Korea **Chōsen** 朝鮮 *or* **Kankoku** 韓国
Korean (language) **Chōsen-go** 朝鮮語
Korean *(person)* **Chōsen-jin** 朝鮮人
Kurile Islands **Chishima Rettō** 千島列島

L

labor *see* work
lace *see* shoelace
lacquer **urushi** 漆; *(lacquer ware)* **nurimono**
塗物; *(raised lacquer)* **maki-e** 蒔絵
ladder **hashigo** はしご
lady **fujin** 婦人
lake **mizuumi** 湖
lamb *(meat)* **yōniku** 羊肉
lame **chimba** ちんば
lamp **rampu** ランプ
land *see* country; *see* earth; *see* place; *(comes
ashore)* **jōriku shimas'** *(suru, sh'te)* 上陸
する; *(from the air)* **chakuriku shimas'**
(suru, sh'te) 着陸する
landlord **shujin** 主人
language **kotoba** ことば *or* **gengo** 言語
lantern *(of paper)* **chōchin** 提灯
lap **hiza** 膝
large *see* big; *see* wide
large-size (model) **ōgata** 大型
last *(final)* **owari no** 終りの *or* **saigo no**
最後の; *(preceding)* **kono mae no** この前の

last night **kinō no ban** (*or* **sakuban**) 昨(日
  の)晩 *or* **yūbe** ゆうべ   「rete) 遅れる
late **osoi** 遅い *or* **okuremas'** (*okureru, oku-*
latrine *see* toilet
laugh **waraimas'** (*warau, waratte*) 笑う
laundry **sentaku** 洗濯
lavatory *see* bathroom; *see* toilet
lawn **shibafu** 芝生
lawn mower **shiba-kari** 芝刈
lawyer **bengoshi** 弁護士
lay (*put*) **okimas'** (*oku, oite*) 置く; (*lie down*)
  nemas' (*neru, nete*) 寝る
lazy (*person*) **namake-mono** なまけもの
lead (*metal*) **namari** 鉛   「案内する
lead (*guide*) **annai shimas'** (*suru, sh'te*)
leaf **happa** 葉っぱ
leak **morimas'** (*moru, motte*) 漏る
learn **naraimas'** (*narau, naratte*) 習う
leave **demas'** (*deru, dete*) 出る; (*for a long
  distance*) **tachimas'** (*tatsu, tatte*) 立つ
lecture **kōgi** 講義
left **hidari** (**no**) 左(の)
leg **ashi** 足   「伝説
legend **mukashi-banashi** 昔話 *or* **densetsu**
leisure **hima** ひま
lemon **remon** レモン
lend **kashimas'** (*kasu, kash'te*) 貸す
lens **renzu** レンズ
less (**yori**) **s'kunai** (より)少ない

lesson **ka** 課; *(takes lessons)* **naraimas'** *(narau, naratte)* 習う

let **sasemas'** *(saseru, sasete)* させる *or* **yurushimas'** *(yurusu, yurush'te)* 許す

let out *(of vehicle)* **oroshimas'** (orosu, orosh'te) 下ろす

letter **tegami** 手紙; *(of the alphabet, etc.)* ⌊**moji** 文字

lever **teko** てこ

lewd **s'kebē (na)** すけべえ (な)

library *(building)* **toshokan** 図書館; *(room)* ⌊**tosho-shitsu** 図書室

lice **shirami** しらみ

license **menkyo** 免許

lick **namemas'** *(nameru, namete)* 嘗める

lid **f'ta** ふた (蓋)

lie *(falsehood)* **uso** うそ

lie *(down)* **nemas'** *(neru, nete)* 寝る

lieutenant *(1st Lt, Lt JG)* **chū-i** 中尉; *(2nd Lt)* **shō-i** 少尉; *(full navy)* **tai-i** 大尉

life **inochi** 命

lift **agemas'** *(ageru, agete)* 上げる

light *(electric)* **denki** 電気 *or* **dentō** 電燈; *(bright)* **akarui** 明るい

light *(weight)* **karui** 軽い

lighter *(cigarette)* **raitā** ライター ⌈**inadzuma**

lightning **inabikari** いな光 *or* **inazuma**

like *(fond of)* **s'ki des'** 好きです *or* **s'kimas'** *(s'ku, suite)* 好く ⌈**ni nite imas'**

like *(similar to)* **...ni nite imas'** *(iru, ite)*

lily **yuri** ゆり

73

limit **kagiri** 限り

line **sen** 線

linen **ama** あま(亞麻), **rinneru** リンネル

linguistics (*language learning*) **gogaku** 語学; (*science of language*) **gengo-gaku** 言語学

lining **ura** 裏

lion **raion** ライオン *or* **shishi** しし

lip **kuchibiru** 唇

liquid **mizu** 水 *or* **ekitai** 液体

liquor **o-sake** お酒

list (*of items*) **hyō** 表; (*puts in a list*) **hyō ni shimas'** (*suru, sh'te*) 表にする

listen **kikimas'** (*kiku, kiite*) 聞く

literature **bungaku** 文学

little **chiisai** 小さい *or* **chitchai** 小っちゃい

live (*inhabits*) **sunde imas'** (*iru, ite*) 住んでいる; (*exists*) **ikite imas'** (*iru, ite*) 生きている

liver **kimo** 肝 *or* **kanzō** 肝臓; (*as food*) **rebā** レバー

loan *see* lend

lobster **ise-ebi** いせえび

local **chihō no** 地方の; (*of the city*) **machi no** 町の

lock **jō** 錠; (*locks a door*) (**to ni**) **kagi o kakemas'** (*kakeru, kakete*) (戸に)かぎをかける

log **maruta** 丸太

loincloth **fundoshi** ふんどし

lonely **hitori-botchi** 一人ぼっち *or* **sabishii** さびしい

long **nagai** 長い

look **mimas'** (*miru, mite*) 見る

lose **nakushimas'** (*nakusu, nakush'te*) 無くす

or ushinaimas' (*ushinau, ushinatte*) 失う
(gets) lost (michi ni) mayoimas' (*mayou, ma-*
lots tak'san 沢山　　　　　　⌊*yotte*) (道に) 迷う
lotus hasu 蓮　　　　　　　　「はで (な)
loud (*noise*) ōkii 大きい; (*color*) hade (na)
loud-speaker kakusei-ki 拡声器
louse *see* lice　　　　　　　　「*also like*
love ai shimas' (*suru, sh'te*) 愛する; *see*
lover koibito 恋人 *or* ii-hito いい人
low hikui 低い
luck un 運
lucky un ga ii 運がいい
luggage te-nimotsu 手荷物
lumber zaimoku 材木
lump katamari 塊
lunch hiru-gohan 昼御飯
lungs hai 肺
luxury zeitaku 贅沢

M

machine kikai 機械
mad *see* angry; *see* insane
made in Japan Nihon-sei (no) 日本製 (の)
magazine zasshi 雑誌
maid jochū 女中
mail yūbin 郵便
main omo na 主な *or* shuyō na 主要な
major (*army*) shōsa 少佐

make (*do*) **shimas'** (*suru*, *sh'te*) する; (*put together*) **ts'kurimas'** (*ts'kuru*, *ts'kutte*) 作る *or* **koshiraemas'** (*koshiraeru*, *koshi-*
male otoko 男   Lraete) こしらえる
man (*male*) **otoko** 男; (*human*) **hito** 人
manage   **tori-atsukaimas'** (*-atsukau*, *-atsukatte*) 取り扱う   「どうにか (する)
manage (to do) **dō ni ka** (**shimas'**; *suru*, *sh'te*)
Manchuria **Manshū** 満洲
mandarin orange *see* tangerine
manner (of doing) **yarikata** やり方
manners *see* etiquette
manuscript **genkō** 原稿
many **tak'san no** 沢山の *or* **ōku no** 多くの
map **chizu** 地図
maple **momiji** もみじ
March **San-gatsu** 三月
marines **kaiheitai** 海兵隊 *or* **rik'sentai** 陸戦隊
mark **shirushi** (**o ts'kemas'**; *ts'keru*, *ts'kete*)
market **ichi(-ba)** 市(場)   L印 (を付ける)
marriage **kekkon** 結婚
marry **kekkon shimas'** (*suru*, *sh'te*) 結婚する
marvellous **sugoi** すごい   「能面
mask **men** 面; (*used in Noh drama*) **nō-men**
masturbate **shuin o shimas'** (*suru*, *sh'te*) 手淫 をする *or* (*vulgar*) **senzuri o kakimas'** (*kaku*, *kaite*) センズリをかく
mat (*Japanese floor*) **tatami** 畳
match (*for fire*) **matchi** マッチ

76

material *see* cloth

materials **zairyō** 材料 *or* **shiryō** 資料

matter **koto** 事

(It doesn't) matter. **Kamaimasen.**

(What's the) matter? **Dō sh'tan' des' ka?**

May **Go-gatsu** 五月

may *(perhaps)* **...ka mo shiremasen** かも
知れません; *(is OK to)* **...-te mo ii des'**

mayor **shichō** 市長 ㄴ**...てもいいです**

me **watashi** 私 *or* **watak'shi** 私

meal **gohan** ご飯 *or* **shokuji** 食事

meaning **imi** 意味

measure **hakarimas'** *(hakaru, hakatte)* 計る

meat **niku** 肉

medicine **k'suri** 薬 「**yake** 半焼け

medium-rare (meat) **han-nie** 半にえ *or* **han-**

medium-size (model) **chūgata** 中型

meet **...ni aimas'** *(au, atte)* に会う

melon **uri** 瓜

melt *(it melts)* **tokemas'** *(tokeru, tokete)*
溶ける; *(melts it)* **tokashimas'** *(tokasu,*
tokash'te) 溶かす

memory **(mono-)oboe** (もの)覚え

mend **naoshimas'** *(naosu, naosh'te)* 直す

menstruation **gekkei** 月経

mental **seishin (no)** 精神(の)

menu **kondate** 献立

merchant **shōnin** 商人

(It's a) mess! **Taihen des' ne.** 大変ですね

77

message **kotozuke** 言づけ

messy **kitanai** きたない

metal **kane** 金

method **shikata** 仕方 *or* **hōhō** 方法

middle **mannaka** まん中

midnight **ma-yonaka** 真夜中

might *see* perhaps

milk **miruku** ミルク, **gyūnyū** 牛乳

million **hyaku-man** 百万

mind **kokoro** 心 *or* **seishin** 精神

(Never) mind. **Kamaimasen.** かまいません

mine (*my*) **watashi no** 私の

minister (*pastor*) **bok'shi** 牧師

minute **fun** 分 (1 **ip-pun**, 3 **sam-pun**, 4 **yom-pun**, 6 **rop-pun**, 8 **hap-pun**)

mirror **kagami** 鏡

Miss . . . . . . **san** さん

miss (*long for*) (**...ga**) **natsukashii** なつかしい

missionary **senkyōshi** 宣教師

mistake **machigai** 間違

mix (*mixes it*) **mazemas'** (*mazeru, mazete*) 混ぜる; (*it mixes*) **mazarimas'** (*mazaru, mazatte*) 混ざる; **majirimas'** (*majiru, majitte*) 混じる

modern **gendai no** 現代の

modest *see* humble

(just a) moment **chotto** ちょっと

Monday **getsuyōbi** 月曜日

money (**o-**)**kane** (お)金

monkey **saru** さる

78

month **ts'ki** 月; (*in counting*) **-kagetsu** 箇月

mood **kibun** 気分

moon **ts'ki** 月 *or* **ots'ki-sama** お月様

mop **moppu** モップ

more **motto** もっと *or* **mō s'koshi** もう少し

morning **asa** 朝

mosquito **ka** か (蚊)

mosquito net **kaya** かや

moss **koke** こけ

most . . . **ichiban** . . . 一番

most of . . . **. . . no daibubun** の大部分

moth **shimi** しみ (衣魚) *or* **mushi** 蛾

moth balls **naf'tarin** ナフタリン *or* **shimi-yoke** しみよけ

mother **okāsan** お母さん *or* **haha** 母

motor **hatsudōki** 発動機

motorcycle **ōtobai** オートバイ

mountain **yama** 山

mouse **hatsuka-nezumi** 二十日ねずみ

mousetrap **nezumi-tori** ねずみとり

mouth **kuchi** 口

move (*it moves*) **ugokimas'** (*ugoku, ugoite*)
  動く; (*moves it*) **ugokashimas'** (*ugokasu,*
  ugokash'te) 動かす

movies **eiga** 映画

movie theater **eiga-kan** 映画館

Mr, Mrs . . . **. . . san** さん

much *see* lots

mud **doro** 泥

murder *see* kill

museum **hakubutsu-kan** 博物館; (*art gallery*) **bijutsu-kan** 美術館

mushroom **kinoko** きのこ (*the most popular kinds are* mats'take まつたけ [松茸] *and* shiitake しいたけ [椎茸])

music **ongaku** 音楽

must **-nakereba narimasen** なければなりません

mustache **kuchi-hige** 口ひげ

mustard **karashi** からし

must not **-te wa ikemasen** てはいけません

mutton *see* lamb

my **watashi no** 私の

myself *see* me

mysterious **fushigi (na)** 不思議 (な)

N

nail **kugi** 釘; (*finger, toe*) **tsume** 爪

naked **hadaka (no)** 裸 (の)

name **namae** 名前

napkin **napukin** ナプキン

narrow **semai** 狭い

natural, nature **shizen (no)** 自然 (の)

naughty **wampaku (na)** わんぱく (な)

navel **heso** へそ

navy **kaigun** 海軍

near **chikai** 近い

nearly **hotondo** ほとんど

necessary **hitsuyō (na)** 必要 (な)

neck **kubi** 首

necklace **kubi-kazari** 頸飾り

necktie **nekutai** ネクタイ

need (...ga) **irimas'** (*iru, itte*) 要る

needle **hari** 針

Negro **Kokujin** 黒人

neighbor(ing) **tonari** 隣

neither ... nor ... **... mo ... mo** (+NEGATIVE)

nephew **oi** おい (甥) *or* **oigo san** おいごさん

nerve **shinkei** 神経

nervous *see* worried

nest **su** 巣

net **ami** 網

never **kessh'te** けっして

new **atarashii** 新しい

news **nyūsu** ニュース

newspaper **shimbun** 新聞

(Happy) New Year! **Shinnen omedetō.** 「おめでとう 新年

next **tsugi** (**no**) 次 (の)

nice *see* good

niece **mei** めい (姪) *or* **meigo san** めいごさん

night **yoru** 夜

nightingale **uguisu** うぐいす

nine **kyū** *or* **ku** 九 *or* **kokonotsu** 九つ

nineteen **jū kyū** *or* **jū ku** 十九

ninety **kyū-jū** *or* **ku-jū** 九十

no **iie** いいえ

nobody **dare mo** + NEGATIVE 誰も

noise **oto** 音; (*boisterous*) **sawagi** 騒ぎ

none (*thing*) **hitotsu mo** + NEGATIVE 一つも；
  (*person*) **hitori mo** + NEGATIVE 一人も
nonsense baka na koto ばかな事
noodles (**o-**)**soba** (お)そば；(*Japanese style*)
  udon うどん；(*Chinese style*)**rāmen** ラーメン
noodle-shop soba-ya そばや；**udon-ya** うど
noon hiru 昼；(*exact time*) **shōgo** 正午 んや
north kita 北
nose hana 鼻
not VERB NEGATIVE (**-nai** *or* **-anai**)
note *see* **letter**
nothing nani mo + NEGATIVE 何も
notice ...ni ki ga ts'kimas' (*ts'ku, tsuite*)
novel shōsetsu 小説   に気が付く
November Jūichi-gatsu 十一月
now ima 今；(*just ...*) **tadaima** 只今
nowhere doko ni mo + NEGATIVE
(gets) **numb shibiremas'** (*shibireru, shibirete*)
number kazu 数   しびれる
nun ama 尼
nurse kangofu 看護婦
nut kenka 堅果
nylon nairon ナイロン

O

obey (*a person*) (**...no**) **yū koto o kikimas'**
  (*kiku, kiite*) 言う事を聞く
object (*thing*) **mono** 物；(*goal*) **mokuteki** 目的

obtain *see* get

occasion **toki** 時; (*circumstance*) **ba(w)ai** 場合

Occident **Seiyō** 西洋

occupation (*job*) **shokugyō** 職業; (*of a country*) **senryō** 占領

occupied (*toilets, etc.*) **shiyō-chū** 使用中; (*telephone*) **hanashi-chū** 話中; (*seat*) **kimas'** 來ます; *see also* busy

occur **okorimas'** (*okoru, okotte*) 起る

ocean **taiyō** 大洋

o'clock **-ji** 時

October **Jū-gatsu** 十月

octopus **tako** たこ

oculist **me-isha** 目医者

odd **hen** (**na**) 変 (な)

of... ...**no** の 「(*kesu, kesh'te*) 消す
(turn) off (*lights, radio, etc.*) (...**o**) **keshimas'**

office **jimusho** 事務所

office worker **jimuin** 事務員

(an) official **yakunin** 役人

often **yoku** よく *or* **tabitabi** 度々

oil **abura** 油 *or* (*for machines, etc.*) **sekiyu** 石油; (*lubricating, for cars*) **oiru** オイル

ointment **nuri-gusuri** 塗薬 「**totta** 年取った

old (*not new*) **furui** 古い; (*not young*) **toshi-**

older **toshi-ue** (**no**) 年上 (の)

olive **oriibu** オリーブ

omelet **omuretsu** オムレツ

omit **otoshimas'** (*otosu, otosh'te*) 落す

on ... ni に or ...no ue ni の上に

(turn) on (*lights, radio, etc.*) (... o) ts'kemas' (*ts'keru, ts'kete*) 付ける

once ichi-do 一度 or ik-kai 一回

one ichi 一 or hitotsu 一つ; (*person*) hitori 「一人

oneself jibun 自分

onion negi ねぎ

only tada ... 只; ...dake だけ

open (*opens it*) akemas' (*akeru, akete*) 開ける; (*it opens*) akimas' (*aku, aite*) 開く

operation shujutsu 手術

opinion iken 意見 or kangae 考え

opium ahen あへん

opportunity kikai 機会

opposite (*facing*) mukō (no) 向う(の); (*contrary*) gyaku (no) 逆(の)

or ka か or mata wa 又は

orange orenji オレンジ; *see also* tangerine

order (*clothes, meal etc.*) chūmon shimas' (*suru, sh'te*) 注文する; (*a person to do something*) ...ni ii-ts'kemas' (*-ts'keru, -ts'kete*) に言いつける

ordinary futsū no 普通の 「dantai 団体

organization (*setup*) sosh'ki 組織; (*group*)

Orient Tōyō 東洋

originally moto wa 元は

ornament kazari 飾り

orphan koji 孤児

orphanage koji-in 孤児院

other **hoka no** 外の *or* **betsu no** 別の
otherwise **sa-mo-nakereba** *or* **sō ja nai to**
ought to ... **sh'ta hō ga ii deshō** *or* ... **suru**
our(s) **watashi-tachi no** 私達の **beki des'**
out **soto e** 外へ; (*is away from home*) **rusu**
outdoors **soto (de)** 外 (で) **des'** 留守です
outside of (*other than*) ... **no hoka** の外
oven **tempi** 天火 *or* **kama** かま
over (*above*) ... **no ue ni** の上に
over (*finished*) (...**o**) ...**-te shimatta** しまった *or* (...**o**) ...**shichatta** しちゃった
over (do, etc.) (**shi-**)**sugimas'** (*sugiru, sugite*) (し)すぎる
overshoes **amagutsu** 雨靴 *or* **ōbāshūzu** 「オーバーシューズ
owing to *see* because
owl **fukuro** ふくろ (梟)
own(*possess*)**motte imas'** (*iru, ite*) 持っている; (*one's*) **jibun no** 自分の
oyster **kaki** かき (牡蠣)

P

Pacific Ocean **Taiheiyō** 太平洋
pack (one's bags) **ni-zukuri o shimas'** (*suru, sh'te*) 荷造をする
package **kozutsumi** 小包
page **pēji** ページ
pain **itami** 痛み 「キ(を塗る)
paint **penki** (o nurimas'; *nuru, nutte*) ペン

85

pair *see* two

palace (*in Tokyo*) **kyūjō** 宮城; (*in Kyoto*) **gosho** 御所

pan **nabe** 鍋

pantry **shokki-shitsu** 食器室

pants **zubon** ズボン; (*underpants*) **zubonsh'ta** ズボン下

paper **kami** 紙; (*newspaper*) **shimbun** 新聞

paradise **tengoku** 天国

paralysis **mahi** まひ

parcel **kozutsumi** 小包

Pardon me. **Shitsurei.** 失礼 *or* **Sumimasen.** すみません *or* **Gomen kudasai.** 御免下さい

paregoric **geri-dome** 下痢止め

parent **oya** 親

parents **ryōshin** 両親

park **kōen** 公園

parrot **ōmu** おうむ

part **bubun** 部分 *or* (*one*) **ichi-bu** 一部

particular **tokubetsu no** 特別の

partner **aite** 相手

party **enkai** 宴会 *or* **pātē** パーテー

pass (*hand around—at table*) **mawashimas'** (*mawasu, mawash'te*) 回す; (*hand over*) **watashimas'** (*watasu, watash'te*) 渡す; (*go past*) **...o tōrimas'** (*tōru, tōtte*) を通る

passport **ryoken** 旅券 *or* **pas'pōto** パスポート

past **kako** 過去

paste **nori** (**o ts'kemas'**; *ts'keru, ts'kete*) のり (を附ける)

pastry **o-kashi** お菓子

patch **tsugimas'** (*tsugu, tsuide*) 継ぐ

path **komichi** 小路
patience **gaman** 我慢
pawnshop **shichi-ya** 質屋
pay (out) **haraimas'** or **shi-haraimas'**
peace **heiwa** 平和 └(*harau, haratte*) (支)払う
peach **momo** 桃
pear **nashi** 梨
pearl **shinju** 真珠
peas **endō(-mame)** えんどう(豆)
peel (...no) **kawa o mukimas'** (*muku*,
Peking **Pekin** ペキン └*muite*) 皮をむく
pen **pen** ペン; (*fountain*) **mannen-hitsu**
pencil **empitsu** 鉛筆 └万年筆
people **hito** 人 or **hitobito** 人々
pepper **koshō** 胡椒
percent **pāsento** パーセント ┌全く(の)
perfect **kanzen** (na) 完全(な) or **mattaku** (no)
perfume **kōsui** 香水 ┌せん or **tabun** 多分
perhaps **...ka mo shiremasen** かもしれま
permanent (wave) **pāma** パーマ
person **hito** 人
perspire *see* sweat
petrol *see* gas(oline)
phone *see* telephone
phonograph **chikuonki** 蓄音器
photograph **shashin** 写真
pick *see* choose
pickpocket **suri** すり
pick up **hiroimas'** (*hirou, hirotte*) 拾う

87

picnic **ensoku** 遠足

picture **e** 絵

(one) piece **(ik-)ko** (一)個 *or* **(hito)tsu** (一)つ;
  (*cut off something*) **hito-kire** 一切れ

pig **buta** 豚

pigeon **hato** はと

(one) pile **(hito-)yama** (一)山

piles *see* hemorrhoids

pill **gan-yaku** 丸薬

pillow **makura** 枕

pimp **pombiki** ポン引き

pimple **nikibi** にきび

pin (*for hair*) **pin** ピン; (*for sewing*) **hari** 針

pinch **tsunerimas'** (*tsuneru, tsunette*) 抓る

pine (*tree*) **matsu** 松

pink **momo-iro** 桃色 *or* **pinku** ピンク

pipe **paipu** パイプ

pitiful **kawaisō (na)** かわいそう(な)

place **tokoro** 所

plain (*not gaudy*) **jimi (na)** じみ(な)

plan **keikaku** 計画; (*intention*) **tsumori** つも

plant **uemas'** (*ueru, uete*) 植える   り

plate **sara** 皿

platform (*at station*) **hōmu** ホーム

play **asobimas'** (*asobu, asonde*) 遊ぶ

play (*drama*) **shibai** 芝居

pleasant **tanoshii** 楽しい

Please. **Dōzo.** どうぞ *or* **...-te kudasai.**
  下さい *or* **Onegai shimas'.** お願いします

plenty **tak'san** 沢山

. . .p.m. **gogo** . . . 午後

pocket **poketto** ポケット

Pocketbook *see* purse

point **ten** 点

point at **sashimas'** (*sasu, sash'te*) 指す

poison **doku** 毒

pole (*rod*) **bō** 棒 *or* **sao** 竿

police **keisatsu** 警察

policeman **omawari-san** お巡りさん *or* **junsa** 「巡査

polish **migakimas'** (*migaku, migaite*) 磨く

polite **teinei (na)** 丁寧(な)

politics **seiji** 政治

pond **ike** 池

poor (*needy*) **bimbō (na)** 貧乏(な); (*unskilful*)
  heta (na) 下手(な); (*bad*) **warui** 悪い

popular **ninki ga arimas'** (*aru, atte*) 人気が
  ある *or* **hayarimas'** (*hayaru, hayatte*) はや
  る 「しる

population **jinkō** 人口

porcelain **jiki** 磁器

porch **genkan** 玄関

pork **buta-niku** 豚肉

pork cutlet **ton-katsu** 豚カツ

pornography **shunga** 春画

port **minato** 港 「**puruman** プルマン

porter (*redcap*) **akabō** 赤帽; (*pullman*)

position *see* place; *see* job

possess *see* own

possible **dekimas'** (*dekiru, dekite*) 出来る

post card **hagaki** 葉書; (*picture post card*)
  e-hagaki 絵葉書

post office **yūbin kyoku** 郵便局

pot **hachi** 鉢

potato (*Irish*) **jagaimo** じゃがいも; (*sweet*)
  imo いも *or* satsuma-imo さつまいも;
  (*baked sweet potato*) yaki-imo 焼いも

pottery **yakimono** 焼物 *or* tōki 陶器

pound (*weight or money*) **pondo** ポンド

pour **tsugimas'** (*tsugu, tsuide*) *or* sosogimas' (*sosogu, sosoide*) 注ぐ

powder (*face*) **oshiroi** おしろい

power **chikara** 力

practice (*drill*) **renshū** 練習

pray **inorimas'** (*inoru, inotte*) 祈る 「ん」

preacher (*Protestant*) **bokushi** (san) 牧師 (さ

prefer ...**no hō ga s'ki des'** の方が好きです

pregnancy **ninshin** 妊娠

pregnant **ninshin (shimas'**; *suru, sh'te*) 妊娠

preparation(s) **jumbi** 準備   L(する)

prescription **shohō** 処方

present (*gift*) **okurimono** 贈り物 *or* pure-
  zento プレゼント; (*as souvenir*) omiyage
  おみやげ

president (*of a nation*) **daitōryō** 大統領

press (on) **oshimas'** (*osu, osh'te*) 押す

pretty **kirei (na)** きれい (な)   「をする

prevent **jama o shimas'** (*suru, sh'te*) じゃま

price **nedan** 値段

priest **shimpu (san)** 神父(さん)

prime minister **shusō** 首相

prison *see* jail

private (use) **shiyō (no)** 私用 (の); (*undisturbed*) **jama sarenai** じゃまされない

probably **tabun** 多分 *or* **osoraku** 恐らく *or ...* (suru) **deshō** (する) でしょう

problem **mondai** 問題

produce (...ga) **dekimas'** (*dekiru, dekite*) 出来る *or* (...o) **tsukurimas'** (*tsukuru, tsukutte*) 作る

professor **kyōju** 教授

promise **yak'soku (shimas'; suru, sh'te)** 約束 (する)

pronunciation **hatsuon** 発音

propaganda **senden** 宣伝

proper **tekitō (na)** 適当 (な)

prostitute **jorō** 女郎

protect **mamorimas'** (*mamoru, mamotte*) 守る

proud of (...o) **jiman shimas'** (*suru, sh'te*) 自慢する

province (*of Japan*) **ken** 県

public **kōshū (no)** 公衆(の)

pull **hipparimas'** (*hipparu, hippatte*) 引張る *or* **hikimas'** (*hiku, hiite*) 引く

pure **junsui (na)** 純粋 (な)

purple **murasaki (no)** 紫 (の)

purpose (*intention*) **tsumori** つもり; (*goal*) **mokuteki** 目的; (on) purpose **waza to** わざと

purse **saifu** *or* **gamaguchi** がまぐち

pus **umi** 膿 (うみ)

push **oshimas'** (*osu, osh'te*) 押す

put **okimas'** (*oku, oite*) 置く
puzzle **nazo** なぞ

Q

quality **hinshitsu** 品質
quantity **ryō** 量
quarrel **kenka** (shimas'; *suru, sh'te*) けんか
queen **joō** 女王
queer **hen (na)** 変(な) *or* **okashii** おかしい
question **shitsumon** 質問
quick **hayai** 早い; (*quickly*) **hayaku** 早く
quiet **shizuka (na)** 静か(な)
quilt **futon** ふとん
quit **yamemas'** (*yameru, yamete*) 止める
quite **sōtō** 相当 *or* **daibu** 大分

R

rabbit **usagi** うさぎ
race **kyōsō** 競争; (*cycles*) **keirin** 競輪; (*horse*) **keiba** 競馬
race track **keiba-jō** 競馬場
race (*peoples*) **jinshu** 人種; (*human*) **jinrui** 人類
radiator (*in house, etc.*) **dambō(-sōchi)** 媛房(装置)
radio **rajio** ラジオ
radish (*Japanese*) **daikon** 大根
raft **ikada** 筏
rag **boro** ぼろ

ragpicker **kuzu-hiroi** くず拾い *or* **batata**
しばたや

railroad **tetsudō** 鉄道

railroad station **eki** 駅

rain **ame** 雨; (*it rains*) **ame ga furimas'**
(*furu, futte*) 雨が降る

rainy season **tsuyu** 梅雨 *or* **nyūbai** 入梅

raise **agemas'** (*ageru, agete*) 上げる

range (*kitchen*) **kamado** かまど; (*gas*) **gasu**
renji ガス・レンジ

rapid *see* fast

rare (*infrequent*) **mare** (**na**) 稀(な); (*not cooked*) **nama no** なま; *see also* (under) done

rat **nezumi** ねずみ

rather **mushiro** むしろ

raw **nama** (**de**) 生(で)

razor **kamisori** かみそり

razor blade **kamisori no ha** かみそりの刃

reach *see* arrive

read **yomimas'** (*yomu, yonde*) 読む いる

ready **dekite imas'** *or* **dekimash'ta** 出来て

real **hontō no** ほんとうの

really **hontō ni** ほんとうに

reason **wake** わけ *or* **riyū** 理由

receipt **uketori** 受取

receive **moraimas'** (*morau, moratte*) 貰う

recently **saikin** 最近 *or* **kono goro** 此頃

record (*phonograph*) **rekōdo** レコード

red **akai** 赤い

reduction *see* discount

refreshments (*food*) **tabemono** 食べ物;

93

(*drink*) **nomimono** 飲物; (*tea*) **ocha** お茶

refrigerator **reizōko** 冷蔵庫　　　　「断る

refuse **kotowarimas'** (*kotowaru, kotowatte*)

Regards to... ...**ni yorosh'ku** (**negai-mas'**). によろしく（願います）

region **chihō** 地方

registered (mail) **kaki-tome** 書留

regular **futsū no** 普通の

relation(ship) **kankei** 関係

relative **shinrui** 親類 *or* **shinseki** 親戚

religion **shūkyō** 宗教

remain **nokorimas'** (*nokoru, nokotte*) 残る; (*stay*) **imas'** (*iru, ite*) 居る *or* **ikimasen** (*ikanai, ikanai de*) 行かない　　「思い出す

remember **omoi-dashimas'** (-*dasu, -dash'te*)

reminds one of **omowasemas'** (*omowaseru, omowasete*) 思わせる

remove **torimas'** (*toru, totte*) 取る

rent (*cost*) **yachin** 家賃; (*rents to*) **kashimas'** (*kasu, kash'te*) 貸す; (*rents from*) **karimas'** (*kariru, karite*) 借りる

(house for) rent **kashiya** 貸家

(rooms for) rent **kashima** 貸間

repair **naoshimas'** (*naosu, naosh'te*) 直す

repeat **mō ichido** (**iimas'**; *yū, itte or yutte*) もう一度（言う）

reporter (**shimbun-**)**kisha** (新聞)記者

request **negaimas'** (*negau, negatte*) 願う *or* **tanomimas'** (*tanomu, tanonde*) 頼む

require *see* need

reservation **yoyaku** 予約 *or* **mōshikomi** 申込

resign **jishoku shimas'** (*suru, sh'te*) 辞職する

respect **sonkei (shimas'**; *suru, sh'te*) 尊敬す

responsibility **sekinin** 責任 └る

rest **yasumimas'** (*yasumu, yasunde*) 休む

rest (*remainder*) **nokori** 残り *or* **hoka** 外

restaurant **res'toran** レストラン *or* **shokudō**

restless **ochits'kanai** 落着かない └食堂

result **kekka** 結果

retail **ko-uri** 小売 ┌(*suru, sh'te*) 退職する

retire (from business) **taishoku shimas'**

return (*home*) **kaerimas'** (*kaeru, kaette*) 帰
る; (*come back where one is now*) **itte
kimas'** (*kuru, kite*) 行って来ます

Reverend... ...**Bok'shi san** 牧師さん *or*
...**Shimpu san** 神父さん

reward **hōbi** ほうび

ribbon **himo** ひも *or* **ribon** リボン

rice (*cooked*) **gohan** 御飯 *or* **meshi** 飯; (*at
store*) **o-kome** お米; (*hulled*) **kome** 米;
(*plants in field*) **ine** いね

rich **kanemochi (no)** 金持(の)

ricksha **jinrikisha** 人力車 *or* **kuruma** 車 (*but
take a taxi; rickshas went out of style with
Mme. Butterfly*)

ride ...**ni norimas'** (*noru, notte*) *or* ...**ni
notte ikimas'** (*iku, itte*) に乗って行く

rifle **shōjū** 小銃

right (*not left*) **migi** 右; (*correct*) **tadashii** 正しい *or* **ii** いい

ring (*on finger*) **yubiwa** 指輪

ring (*like a bell*) **narimas'** (*naru, natte*) 鳴る

ripe **jukush'ta** 熟した

rise (*get up*) **okimas'** (*okiru, okite*) 起きる; (*go up*) **agarimas'** (*agaru, agatte*) 上がる *or* (*sun, climb*) **noborimas'** (*noboru, nobotte*) 昇る

river **kawa** 川

road **michi** 道

roast beef **rōsu(-biifu)** ロース(ビーフ)

rob *see* steal

robber **dorobō** 泥棒

rock **ishi** 石 *or* **iwa** 岩

roll **korogarimas'** (*korogaru, korogatte*) ころがる

roof **yane** 屋根

room **heya** 部屋

root **ne** 根

rope **nawa** 縄 *or* **tsuna** 綱

rose **bara** ばら

rot **k'sarimas'** (*k'saru, k'satte*) 腐る

rough **arai** 粗い

round **marui** 円い

row (*a boat*) **kogimas'** (*kogu, koide*) 漕ぐ

rub **kosurimas'** (*kosuru, kosutte*) 擦る

rubber **gomu** ゴム

rude **burei (na)** 無礼(な)

rug **shikimono** 敷物 *or* **jūtan** じゅうたん

ruin **dame ni shimas'** (*suru, sh'te*) 駄目にする

rumor uwasa うわさ

run hashirimas' (*hashiru, hashitte*) 走る *or* kakemas' (*kakeru, kakete*) 駆ける

rush isogimas' (*isogu, isoide*) 急ぐ

Russia Roshiya ロシヤ *or* Soren ソ連

rust sabi さび

S

sack fukuro 袋

sad kanashii 悲しい

saddle kura 鞍

safe(ly) buji (ni) 無事(に)

safety pin anzem-pin 安全ピン

sail ho 帆

sailor funanori 船乗り *or* suifu 水夫; (*member of crew*) sen-in 船員; (*naval enlisted man*) suihei 水兵

sake of . . . . . . no tame (ni) の為(に)

saké (rice wine) (o-)sake (お)酒

salad sarada サラダ

salary hōkyū 俸給 *or* kyūryō 給料; (*monthly*) gekkyū 月給

saliva tsubaki つばき(唾)

salmon sake さけ(鮭)

salt shio 塩

same onaji 同じ

sample mihon 見本

sand suna 砂

sandal sandaru サンダル

sandwich **sando(-witchi)** サンド（ウィッチ）

sanitary **eisei-teki (na)** 衛生的（な）

sanitary belt **gekkei-tai** 月経帯

sarcasm **hiniku** 皮肉

sardine **iwashi** いわし

satin **shusu** しゅす

satisfied **manzoku shimas'** (*suru, sh'te*) 満足

Saturday **doyōbi** 土曜日

sauce **sōsu** ソース

saucer **ko-zara** 小皿, **uke-zara** 受皿

save (*time, etc.*) **ken-yaku shimas'** (*suru,*

saw **nokogiri** のこぎり　　　⌊*sh'te*) 倹約する

say (that...) (...to) **iimas'** (*yū, itte or*

scarce **s'kunai** 少い　　　　⌊*yutte*) （と）言う

scenery **kesh'ki** 景色

schedule (*train*) **daiya** ダイヤ; (*the timetable itself*) **jikan-hyō** 時間表

scholar **gak'sha** 学者

school **gakkō** 学校

science **kagaku** 科学

scissors **hasami** 鋏

scold **sh'karimas'** (*sh'karu, sh'katte*) 叱る

scrambled eggs **s'kuramburu-eggu** スクランブル・エッグ

scratch **kakimas'** (*kaku, kaite*) 掻く

screen (*folding*) **byōbu** びょうぶ

screw **neji** ねじ

screwdriver **neji-mawashi** ねじ回し

scroll **makimono** 巻物

sea **umi** 海　　　「in 印

seal (*for stamping one's name*) **han** 判 *or*

search for **sagashimas'** (*sagasu, sagash'te*)

seasickness **funa-yoi** 船酔　　└探す

season **kisetsu** 季節

seasoning (*food*) **chōmi** 調味 *or* **aji** 味

seat **koshi-kake** こしかけ *or* **zaseki** 座席 *or* **seki** 席

second **futatsu-me no** 二つ目の *or* **ni-bamme no** 二番目の

second class **ni-tō** 二等　　「古い

secondhand **chūburu no** 中古の *or* **furui**

secret **himitsu** 秘密

secretary **shoki** 書記

see **mimas'** (*miru, mite*) 見る

seed **tane** 種

seek *see* search for

seems like ...**to miemas'** (*mieru, miete*) と見える *or* ...**rashii des'** らしいです

seize **ts'kamimas'** (*ts'kamu, ts'kande*) つかむ *or* **toraemas'** (*toraeru, toraete*) 捕える

seldom **metta ni** ... + NEGATIVE めったに *or* **hotondo** + NEGATIVE 殆ど

select *see* choose

self **jibun** 自分

selfish **wagamama** わがまま

sell **urimas'** (*uru, utte*) 売る

send **okurimas'** (*okuru, okutte*) 送る; (*a telegram*) **uchimas'** (*utsu, utte*) 打つ; (*a*

99

person) **ikasemas'** (*ikaseru, ikasete*) 行か
└せる

sense *see* feel

sentence (*written*) **bunshō** 文章; (*spoken*)
koto こと

separate (*different*) **betsu (no)** 別の; (*separates them*) **wakemas'** (*wakeru, wakete*)
分ける; (*they separate*) **wakaremas'** (*wakareru, wakarete*) 分れる

September **Ku-gatsu** 九月

sergeant **gunsō** 軍曹

serious **majime (na)** まじめ(な)

servant **meshits'kai** 召使い; **shiyōnin** 使用人

serve (*a meal*) **dashimas'** (*dasu, dash'te*)
出す

service (*in restaurant, etc.*) **sābisu** サービス

sesame **goma** ごま 「セット; *see also* sit

set **okimas'** (*oku, oite*) 置く; (*hair*) **setto**

set (*collection*) (**hito-**)**kumi** (一)組 「定める

settle (*decide*) **kimemas'** (*kimeru, kimete*)

seven **nana** *or* **shichi** 七 *or* **nanatsu** 七つ

seventeen **jū nana** *or* **jū shichi** 十七

seventy **nana-jū** *or* **shichi-jū** 七十 「若干

several **f'tatsu-mitsu** 二つ三つ *or* **jakkan**

sew **nuimas'** (*nuu, nutte*) 縫う

sewing machine **mishin** ミシン

sex **sei** 性

(has) sex **yarimas'** (*yaru, yatte*) やる

shade **kage** 蔭

shadow **kagebōshi** 影法師

100

shake (*shakes it*) **furimas'** (*furu, futte*) 振る;
(*it shakes*) **furuemas'** (*furueru, furuete*)
震える 「suru, etc.」

shall USE PRESENT TENSE (**shimas',**
shame **hazukashii koto** はずかしいこと
(That's a) shame. **Sore wa ikemasen ne.**

shape **katachi** 形 「*see also* divide, Dutch
(one's) share (of expenses) **dashi-mae** 出し前;

shark **same** さめ

sharp **surudoi** 鋭い 「そる

shave **hige o sorimas'** (*soru, sotte*) ひげを

she **kano-jo** 彼女 *or* **ano hito** あの人

shed **mono-oki** 物置

sheep **hitsuji** 羊

sheet (*of paper, etc.*) (**ichi-**)**mai** (一)枚

sheets (*for bed*) **shiitsu** シーツ

shelf **tana** 棚

shell **kara** 殼

shine (*it shines*) **hikarimas'** (*hikaru, hikatte*)
光る; (*shines it*) **migakimas'** (*migaku,*
ship **fune** 船 *migaite*) 磨く

shirt **wai-shatsu** ワイシャツ; (*undershirt*)
shatsu シャツ

shoe **kutsu** 靴

shoe box **geta-bako** 下駄箱

shoehorn **kutsu-bera** 靴べら

shoelaces **kutsu-himo** 靴ひも

shoeshine (man) **kutsu-migaki** 靴磨き

shoot **irimas'** (*iru, itte*) 射る

shop (*store*) **mise** 店

101

shopping **kai-mono** 買物

shore **kishi** 岸 *or* **kaigan** 海岸

short (*not long*) **mijikai** 短い; (*not tall*)

short cut **chika-michi** 近道

should *see* ought

shoulder **kata** 肩

shout (*call out*) **sakebimas'** (*sakebu, sakende*) 叫ぶ; (*speak loudly*) **donarimas'**; (*donaru,*

shovel **shaberu** シャベル ⌊*donatte*) 怒鳴る

show **misemas'** (*miseru, misete*) 見せる; *see also* movie, play

shower (bath) **shawā** シャワー

shrimp(s) **ebi** えび; (*fried in batter, Japanese style*) **ebi-tempura** えび天ぷら; (*fried in bread crumbs, American style*) **ebi-furai** えびフライ

shrine (*Shinto*) (**o-**)**miya** お宮 *or* **jingū** 神宮 *or* **jinja** 神社

shrink **chijimimas'** (*chijimu, chijinde*) 縮む

shut **shimemas'** (*shimeru, shimete*) 締める

shy **uchiki** (**na**) 内気(な); **hanikamimas'** (*hanikamu, hanikande*) はにかむ

Siberia **Shiberiya** シベリヤ

sick **byōki** (**no**) 病気(の); (*feels sick to one's stomach*) **mukats'kimas'** (*mukats'ku, mukatsuite*) むかつく

side **yoko** 横; *or* (*of body*) **waki** わき

(that) side **achira-gawa** あちら側

(this) side **kochira-gawa** こちら側

(which) side **dochira-gawa** どちら側

(both) sides **ryŏ-gawa** 両側

sidewalk **hodō** 歩道 or **jindō** 人道

sieve **furui** ふるい (篩)

sight-seeing **kembutsu** 見物 or **kankō** 観光

sign (board) **kamban** 看板 「**sh'te**」署名する

sign (one's name) **shomei shimas'** (*suru,*

signal **shingō** 信号

silent **damarimas'** (*damaru, damatte*) 黙る

silk **kinu** 絹

silver **gin** 銀

simple **kantan** (na) 簡単 (な)

since (**sono**) **go** (その) 後

sincere **seijitsu** (na) 誠実

sing **utaimas'** (*utau, utatte*) 歌う

single (*for one person*) **hitori no** 一人の;
(*unmarried*) **hitori-mono** ひともの

sink (*in kitchen*) **nagashi** 流し; (*it sinks*)
shizumimas' (*shizumu, shizunde*) 沈む;
(*sinks it*) **shizumemas'** (*shizumeru, shizu-
mete*) 沈める

sister **onna no kyōdai** 女のきょうだい;
(*older*) **ane** 姉 or **nē-san** ねえさん; (*younger*) **imōto(-san)** 妹 (さん)

sit **suwarimas'** (*suwaru, suwatte*) 坐る (*strictly speaking this is Japanese style, but it
is used for both*); (*chair style*) **kosh'-
kakemas'** (*-kakeru, -kakete*) 腰掛ける

six **roku** 六 or **muttsu** 六つ

sixteen **jū roku** 十六

103

sixty **roku-jū** 六十

size **ōkisa** 大きさ

skating **s'kēto** スケート 「(をする)

ski **s'kii (o shimas'; suru, sh'te)** スキー

skin (*of person*) **hifu** 皮膚;(*of animal*) **kawa** 皮

skirt(s) **s'kāto** スカート;(*of mountain*) **suso** 裾

sky **sora** 空

sled **sori** そり

sleep **nemas' (neru, nete)** 寝る or **nemurimas' (nemuru, nemutte)** 眠る

sleepy **nemui** 眠い

sleeve **sode** 袖;(*end of kimono sleeve*)**tamoto** 袂

slender **hosoi** 細い

slice *see* cut; *see* piece

slide, slip **suberimas' (suberu, subette)** 滑る

slippers **surippa** スリッパ or **uwabaki** 上履

slot **kuchi** 口

slow **osoi** 遅い

sly **zurui** ずるい

small *see* little

small-size (model) **kogata** 小型

smell **nioi** におい;(*it smells*) **nioimas' (niou,
motte)** におう or **nioi ga shimas' (suru,
sh'te)** においがする;(*smells it*) **kagimas'
(kagu, kaide)** 嗅ぐ 「にこする

smile **niko-niko shimas' (suru, sh'te)** にこ

smoke **kemuri** 煙;(*smokes a cigarette*) **tabako o nomimas' (nomu, nonde)** タバコ
を呑む or **suimas' (suu, sutte)** 吸う

smooth **nameraka (na)** 滑か (な) or **subekkoi** 滑っこい

snack **oyatsu** おやつ

snake **hebi** 蛇

sneeze **kushami (shimas';** *suru, sh'te)* くしゃみする

snore **ibiki (o kakimas';** *kaku, kaite)* いびき (をかく)

snow **yuki (ga furimas';** *furu, futte)* 雪が降る

so **sō** そう; (much) **sonna ni** そんなに

soap **sekken** 石けん or **shabon** シャボン

socialism **shakai-shugi** 社会主義

society **shakai** 社会, (association) **kyōkai** 協会

socks **kutsu-sh'ta** 靴下

soft **yawarakai** 柔らかい

soil (*earth*) **tsuchi** 土 or **tochi** 土地; (*makes dirty*) **yogoshimas'** (*yogosu, yogosh'te*) よごす; (*gets dirty*) **yogoremas'** (*yogoreru, yogorete*) よごれる

soldier **heitai** 兵隊 [*Japanese*)

solid **katai** 堅い

some (*a little*) **s'koshi** (*but often omitted in Japanese*)

some (*a particular one*) **aru...** ある; (people) **aru hito** ある人

somebody **dare ka** 誰か

something **nani ka** 何か

sometime **itsu ka** いつか

sometimes **toki-doki** 時々

somewhere **doko ka** 何処か [*坊っちゃん*

son **mus'ko** むすこ or (*someone elses*) **bot-chan**

song **uta** 歌

soon **ma-mo-naku** 間もなく or **sugu** すぐ

sore **itai** 痛い

sorry (*for you or him*) **ki no doku des'** 「気の毒です

Sorry! **Sumimasen.** すみません

sort (*kind*) **shurui** 種類

soul *see* spirit

sound (*noise*) **oto** 音

soup **sūpu** スープ; (*Japanese clear*) **sui-mono** 吸物; (*Japanese dark*) **miso-shiru** みそ汁

soup-stock **dashi** 出し

sour **suppai** すっぱい

south **minami** 南

Soviet Union **Soren** ソ連

sow (*seeds*) **makimas'** (*maku, maite*) 蒔く

space (*available*) **ma** 間; (*between two things*) **aida** あいだ

Spain **S'pein** スペイン

Spanish (*language*) **S'pein-go** スペイン語

sparrow **suzume** すずめ

speak **hanashimas'** (*hanasu, hanash'te*) 話す

special **tokubetsu no** 特別の 「**nitō** 特別一等

special 2nd class **toku-ni** 特二 *or* **tokubetsu-**

spectacles *see* glasses

speech **hanashi** 話

speed **hayasa** 速さ *or* **sokudo** 速度 「字を綴る

spell **ji o tsuzurimas'** (*tsuzuru, tsuzutte*)

spend **ts'kaimas'** (*ts'kau, ts'katte*) 使う *or* **dashimas'** (*dasu, dash'te*) 出す

spices **chōmi(-ryō)** 調味(料)

spider **kumo** くも(蜘蛛)

spill **koboshimas'** (*kobosu, kobosh'te*) こぼす

spinach **hōrensō** ほうれんそう

spinning (mill) **bōseki(-kōjō)** 紡績（工場）

spirit **seishin** 精神 *or* **kokoro** 心　「を）吐く

spit (tsuba o) **hakimas'** (*haku, haite*) （つば

(in) spite of . . .(that) (sore). . .(na) **no ni** (それ

splendid **rippa** (na) 立派（な）　　　└な）のに

split (*splits it*) **warimas'** (*waru, watte*) 割る；

(*it splits*) **waremas'** (*wareru, warete*) 割れる

spoil (*spoils it*) **waruku shimas'** (*suru, sh'te*)

　悪くする；(*it spoils*) **waruku narimas'**

sponge **kaimen** 海綿　└(*naru, natte*) 悪くなる

spongecake **kas'tera** カステラ

spoon **s'pūn** スプーン *or* **saji** 匙

sport(s) **s'pōtsu** スポーツ *or* **undō** 運動

spot **ten** 点

spread (*spreads it*) **hirogemas'** (*hirogeru,*
hirogete) 広げる；(*spreads it out*) **nobashi-**
mas' (*nobasu, nobash'te*) 伸ばす；(*it spreads*)
hirogarimas' (*hirogaru, hirogatte*) 広がる；
(*it spreads out*) **nobimas'** (*nobiru, nobite*)

spring (*season*) **haru** 春　　　　　　└伸びる

(hot) spring **onsen** 温泉

spy **s'pai** スパイ

square **sh'kaku** 四角　　　　　　　「しゃがむ

squat **shagamimas'** (*shagamu, shagande*)

squeeze **tsubushimas'** (*tsubusu, tsubush'te*)

　つぶす；(out) **shiborimas'** (*shiboru, shibotte*)

squirrel **risu** りす　　　　　　　　└しぼる

stage **butai** 舞台

stairs **kaidan** 階段 or (*wooden*) **hashigo-dan**
はしご段

stamp (*postal*) **kitte** 切手

stand (up) **tachimas'** (*tatsu, tatte*) 立つ

star **hoshi** 星

start *see* begin

state (of the U.S.) **shū** 州

station (*railroad*) **eki** 駅 ; *see also* gas station

stationery **binsen** 便箋

statue **zō** 像 or (*bronze*) **dōzō** 銅像

stay **imas'** (*iru, ite*) 居る or **todomarimas'**
(*todomaru, todomatte*) 留まる ; (*over night*)
tomarimas' (*tomaru, tomatte*) 泊まる

steal **nusumimas'** (*nusumu, nusunde*) 盗む

steam **jōki** 蒸気 or **yuge** 湯気

steel **hagane** はがね or **kōtetsu** 鋼鉄

step (*walk*) **arukimas'** (*aruku, aruite*) 歩く

stick (*club*) **bō(kkire)** 棒(っきれ) ; (*it sticks
to*) ...**ni kuttsukimas'** (*kuttsuku, kuttsu-
ite*) にくっつく ; (*sticks it on*) **harimas'** (*haru,
hatte*) 貼る

sticky **neba-neba shimas'** (*suru, sh'te*) ねば
「ねばする

still (*yet*) **mada** まだ ; (*but*) **demo** でも

sting **sashimas'** (*sasu, sash'te*) 刺す

stir **kaki-mawashimas'** (*mawasu, mawash'te*)
かき回す

stockings **kutsu-sh'ta** 靴下

stomach **o-naka** おなか or **hara** 腹

stone **ishi** 石

stop (*it comes to rest*) **tomarimas'** (*tomaru,
tomatte*) とまる ; (*it stops*) **yamimas'** (*yamu,*

yande) 止む; *(stops it)* **tomemas'** *(tomeru, tomete)* とめる; *(stops doing it)* **yamemas'** *(yameru, yamete)* 止める

store *(shop)* **mise** 店

storm **arashi** あらし (嵐)

story **hanashi** 話

stove **s'tōbu** ストーブ *or (kitchen)* **kamado** しかまど

straight **massugu (na)** まっすぐ(な)

strange **hen (na)** 変(な)

stranger **shiranai hito** 知らない人

straw **wara** わら

strawberry **ichigo** いちご

street **michi** 道 *or* **shadō** 車道

stretch *(stretches it)* **nobashimas'** *(nobasu, nobash'te)* 伸ばす; *(it stretches)* **nobimas'** *(nobiru, nobite)* 伸びる

strike **s'toraiki** ストライキ; *see also* hit

string *(thread)* **ito** 糸; *(cord)* **himo** ひも

strong **tsuyoi** 強い

student **gak'sei** 学生

study **benkyō shimas'** *(suru, sh'te)* 勉強する

stuff *(thing)* **mono** 物; *(fill)* **tsumemas'** *(tsumeru, tsumete)* つめる

styptic pencil **chi-dome** 血止め

suburb **kōgai** 郊外

subway **chikatetsu** 地下鉄

succeed **seikō shimas'** *(suru, sh'te)* 成功する

such **sonna** そんな

suck **suimas'** *(suu, sutte)* 吸う

suddenly **totsuzen** 突然

sugar **satō** 砂糖

suit **yōf'ku** 洋服

suitable **fusawashii** ふさわしい

suitcase **kaban** かばん

summer **natsu** 夏

sun **o-hi-sama** お日さま *or* **taiyō** 太陽

sun-bathing **hinata-bokko** ひなたぼっこ

Sunday **nichiyōbi** 日曜日

sunshine **hinata** ひなた

supper **ban-gohan** 晩御飯

supply **kyōkyū shimas'** (*suru, sh'te*) 供給する

suppose *see* think

sure **tash'ka (na)** 確か（な）

surprised **bikkuri shimas'** (*suru, sh'te*)
びっくりする *or* **odorokimas'** (*odoroku, odoroite*) 驚く

swallow (*bird*) **tsubame** つばめ

swan **hakuchō** はくちょう

sweat **ase** (*ga demas'; deru, dete*) 汗が出る

sweep **sōji shimas'** (*suru, sh'te*) 掃除する *or*
hakimas' (*haku, haite*) 掃く

sweeper **sōji-ki** 掃除機

sweet (*taste*) **amai** 甘い

sweetheart **ii-hito** いい人 *or* **koibito** 恋人

swell up **haremas'** (*hareru, harete*) 腫る；
ōkiku narimas' (*naru, natte*) 大きくなる

swim **oyogimas'** (*oyogu, oyoide*) 泳ぐ

swim suit *see* bathing suit

swing (back and forth) **yuremas'** (*yureru,* yurete*) ゆれる
sword **katana** 刀
syllable **onsetsu** 音節
syringe (*for injections*) **chūsha-ki** 注射器;
(*for water*) **chūsui-ki** 注水器
syrup **shiroppu** シロップ
system **taikei** 体系 or **seido** 制度

T

table **tēburu** テーブル
table-cloth **tēburu-kake** テーブル掛け
tail **shippo** しっぽ
tailor **shitate-ya** 仕立屋 or **yōf'ku-ya** 洋服屋
take **torimas'** (*toru, totte*) 取る
talk **hanashimas'** (*hanasu, hanash'te*) 話す
tall **takai** 高い
tangerine **mikan** みかん
tape **tēpu** テープ
tape recorder **tēpu-rekōdā** テープ・レコーダー
taste **ajiwaimas'** (*ajiwau, ajiwatte*) 味う;
tattoo **ire-zumi** いれずみ (*flavor*) **aji** 味
tax **zei** 税
taxi **tak'shii** タクシー or **kuruma** 車
tea **cha** 茶; (*green*) **o-cha** お茶;
(*black*) **kōcha** 紅茶
teach **oshiemas'** (*oshieru, oshiete*) 教える
teacher **sensei** 先生
team **chiimu** チーム

111

tear (*in eye*) **namida** 涙

tear (tore, torn) **sakimas'** (*saku, saite*) 裂く
or **yaburimas'** (*yaburu, yabutte*) 破る

tease **ijimemas'** (*ijimeru, ijimete*) いじめる

telegram **dempō** (**o uchimas'**; *utsu, utte*)
電報 (を打つ)   「*kakete*) 電話 (をかける)

telephone **denwa** (**o kakemas'**; *kakeru,*
television **terebi** テレビ

tell **iimas'** (*yū, itte* or *yutte*) 言う

temple (**o-**)**tera** (お)寺

ten **jū** *or* **tō** 十

tent **tento** テント   「**osoroshii** 恐しい

terrible **mono-sugoi** ものすごい; (*frightening*)

terribly **mono-sugoku** ものすごく; (*frighten-*
test **sh'ken** 試験 ⌊*ingly* **osorosh'ku** 恐しく

than... ...**yori** より   「を言う

thank **o-rei o iimas'** (*yū, itte* or *yutte*) お礼

Thank you. **Arigatō (gozaimas').** *or* **Dōmo.**
or **Sumimasen.**   「あの

that... **sono**...その; (*over there*) **ano**...

that (one) **sore** それ; (*over there*) **are** あれ

the *usually not translated*   「**shibai** 芝居

theater (*building*) **gekijō** 劇場; (*play*)

them, they (*people*) **ano hito-tachi** あの人達
or **kare-ra** 彼等; (*things*) **sore-ra** それら

then (*at that time*) **sono toki** その時; (*after
that*) **sore kara** それから; (*in that case*)
sore nara それなら   「あそこ

there **soko** そこ; (*over there*) **as'ko** *or* **asoko**

112

thermos bottle **mahō-bin** まほおびん

these **kore-ra** これら

they *see* them

thick **atsui** 厚い; (and round) **futoi** 太い

thief **dorobō** 泥棒

thimble **yubinuki** 指貫

thin **usui** 薄い; (and round) **hosoi** 細い

thing **mono** もの (物); (*fact*) **koto** こと (事)

think (that...) (...to) **omoimas'** (*omou, omotte*) (と) 思う *or* **kangaemas'** (*kangaeru, kangaete*) 考える 「**me (no)** 三番目 (の)

third **mittsu-me (no)** 三っ目 (の) *or* **sambam-**

third class **san-tō** 三等 「きました

thirsty **nodo ga kawakimash'ta** のどがかわ

thirteen **jū san** 十三

thirty **san-jū** 三十

this... **kono...** この

this (one) **kore** これ

thorn **toge** 刺

those *see* them

though **de mo** でも

thought **kangae** 考

thousand **sen** 千

thousand Yen **sen-en** 千円

thread **ito** 糸

three **san** 三 *or* **mittsu** 三つ

throat **nodo** のど

through (*putting*) **...o tōsh'te** を通して; (*coming*) **...o tōtte** 通って; (*seeing*)...

(no aida) kara (の間)から; (*by means of*)
...**de** で *or* ...**o ts'katte** を使って
through (*finished*) ...**te   shimaimash'ta**
しまいました *or* **dekimash'ta** 出来ました
throw nagemas' (*nageru, nagete*) 投げる
thumb oya-yubi 親指
thunder kaminari かみなり
Thursday mokuyōbi 木曜日
ticket kippu 切符
ticket seller kippu-uri 切符売り   「くすぐる
tickle kusugurimas' (*kusuguru, kusugutte*)
tide shio 潮   「(筋肉)   「*see also* necktie
tie musubimas' (*musubu, musunde*) 結ぶ;
tiger tora 虎   「狭い; *see also* drunk
tight kitsui きつい, **katai** 堅い;(*skimpy*)**semai**
tile (*roof*) **kawara** 瓦; (*floor*) **tairu** タイル
time toki 時; (*hour*) **jikan** 時間; (*free*) **hima**
tin buriki ブリキ   └ひま
tip (*money*) **chippu** チップ *or* **kokorozuke**
tire (*of wheel*) **taiya** タイヤ   └心付け
(gets) tired ts'karemas' (*ts'kareru, ts'karete*)
to ...**ni** に *or* ...**e** へ   └疲れる
tobacco tabako タバコ
today kyō 今日
toe ashi-yubi 足指
together issho ni 一緒に *or* **tomo ni** 供に
toilet benjo 便所
tomorrow ash'ta 明日
tongs (*for fire*) **hi-bashi** 火ばし**

tongue **sh'ta** 舌

tonight **komban** 今晩

too (*also*) **...mo** も

too (*overly*) **ammari** あんまり

tool **dōgu** 道具

tooth **ha** 歯

tooth brush **ha-burashi** 歯ブラシ

toothpaste (*or* powder) **ha-migaki** 歯磨

toothpick **koyōji** 小楊子

top **ue** 上; (*summit*) **chōjō** 頂上

top (*toy*) **koma** こま

toss *see* throw

total **zembu** (**de**) 全部(で)

touch **sawarimas'** (*sawaru, sawatte*) 触る *or*
  (**te o**) **furemas'** (*fureru, furete*) (手を)触
  れる

tough **katai** 堅い

tourist **kankō-kyaku** 観光客

toward **...no hō e** …の方へ

towel **tenugui** 手拭 *or* **taoru** タオル

town **machi** 町

toy **omocha** おもちゃ

trader **shōnin** 商人

traffic **kōtsū** 交通

traffic signal(s) **kōtsū-shingō** 交通信号

train **kisha** 汽車; (*electric*) **densha** 電車

translate **yakushimas'** (*yakusu, yakush'te*)
  訳す

travel **ryokō shimas'** (*suru, sh'te*) 旅行する

tray **obon** お盆

treasure **takara(mono)** 宝(物)

treat (*to food*) **gochisō (shimas'; *suru*, *sh'te*)** ごちそう(する); (*medically*) **chiryō shimas'** (*suru*, *sh'te*) 治療する

tree **ki** 木

trick *see* cheat

trip **ryokō** 旅行

trivial *see* unimportant

trouble (*inconvenience*) **tekazu** or **tesū** 手数 or **meiwaku** 迷惑 or **sewa** 世話; (*difficulty*) **konnan** 困難 or **komaru tokoro** 困ると ころ; *see also* worry

trousers **zubon** ズボン

trout **masu** ます (鱒)

truck **torakku** トラック; (*3-wheeled*) **sanrin-sha** 三輪車

true **honto (no)** ほんと(の)

truly **honto ni** ほんとに or **makoto ni** まことに

trust **shin-yō shimas'** (*suru*, *sh'te*) 信用する

try **yatte mimas'** (*miru*, *mite*) やってみる

tub **oke** 桶

tube **kuda** or **kan** 管

tuberculosis **kekkaku** 結核 or **haibyō** 肺病

Tuesday **kayōbi** 火曜日

tunnel **tonneru** トンネル

Turkey **Toruko** トルコ

turkey **shichimen-chō** しちめんちょう

turn (*change directions*) **magarimas'** (*magaru*, *magatte*) 曲る; (*go round*) **mawarimas'** (*mawaru*, *mawatte*) 回る; (*make go round*) **mawashimas'** (*mawasu*, *mawash'te*) 回す

turtle **kame** かめ (亀)

twelve **jū ni** 十二

twenty **ni-jū** 二十　「(*double*) **ni-bai** 二倍

twice (*two times*) **ni-do** 二度 *or* **ni-kai** 二回;

twins **f'tago** ふたご　　　　　「二人

two **ni** 二 *or* **f'tatsu** 二つ; (*people*) **f'tari**

type(write) **taipu(raitā) de uchimas'** (*utsu, utte*) タイプ(ライター)で打つ

typewriter **taipuraitā** タイプライター

typhoon **taifū** 大風

U

ugly **minikui** 醜い

umbrella **kasa** 傘

unbutton **botan o hazushimas'** (*hazusu, hazush'te*) ボタンをはずす

uncle **oji san** おじさん

uncomfortable **furaku** (na) 不樂(な)

unconcerned *see* calm

under ...**no sh'ta** (ni) の下 (に)　「わかる

understand **wakarimas'** (*wakaru, wakatte*)

underwear **sh'ta-gi** 下着　　　　　「ず す

undo **hazushimas'** (*hazusu, hazush'te*) は

undress **kimono o nugimas'** (*nugu, nuide*)

uniform **seif'ku** 制服　　 ⌊着物を脱ぐ

unimportant (*matter*) **mondai ni naranai** 問題にならない

unless ...(**shi-**)**nakereba** (し)なければ

untie **tokimas'** (*toku, toite*) 解く *or* **hodoki-**

117

 mas' (*hodoku, hodoite*) ほどく
until ... made まで
unusual kawatta 変った
up (... no) ue e 上へ
(go) up agarimas' (*agaru, agatte*) 上る
upon *see* on
upside down sakasama さかさま *or* abekobe
upstairs (o-)nikai (ni) (お)二階(に)
urge susumemas' (*susumeru, susumete*)
urinal (*place*) benjo 便所; (*thing*) shibin 尿瓶
urinate shōben shimas' (*suru, sh'te*) 小便する
urine shōben 小便
us, we watashi-tachi 私達
use ts'kaimas' (*ts'kau, ts'katte*) 使う
used to PAST (sh'ta)+mon' des'
usual futsū no 普通の

V

vacant aite imas' (*iru, ite*) あいている
vacation yasumi 休み
vacuum cleaner shinkū-sōjiki 真空掃除機
vague aimai (na) あいまい(な)
valley tani(ma) 谷間
valuable taisetsu (na) 大切(な)
value neuchi 値打
valve ben 弁
vanish (*from sight*) mienaku narimas'
 (*naru, natte*) 見えなくなる; (*from ex-*

istence) **naku narimas'** *(naru, natte)* 無く
なる　　　　　　　　　「いろんな

various **iroiro (no/na)** 色々 (の/な) *or* **ironna**

vase **bin** びん; *(for flowers)* **kabin** 花びん

vegetable **yasai** 野菜

vehicle **norimono** 乗物 *or* **kuruma** 車

velvet **birōdo** ビロード

venereal disease **seibyō** 性病

verb **dōshi** 動詞

very **taihen** 大変 *or* **hijō ni** 非常に

vest **chokki** チョッキ

view *see* opinion; *see* scenery; *see* look

village **mura** 村

vinegar **su** 酢

violet **sumire** すみれ

virgin *(woman)* **oboko** おぼこ *or* **shojo** 処女:
(man) **dōtei** 童貞

visit **asobi ni ikimas'** *(iku, itte)* 遊びに行く
or **tazunemas'** *(tazuneru, tazunete)* 尋ねる
or **ukagaimas'** *(ukagau, ukagatte)* 伺う

visitor **raikyaku** 来客

vitamin(s) **bitamin** ビタミン

vocabulary **kotoba** ことば *or* **goi** 語彙

voice **koe** 声

volcano **kazan** 火山

vomit **modoshimas'** *(modosu, modosh'te)*
もどす

vote **tōhyō shimas'** *(suru, sh'te)* 投票する

vulgar **gehin (na)** 下品 (な)

119

W

waist **koshi** 腰

wait **machimas'** (*matsu, matte*) 待つ

waiter, waitress **kyūji** 給仕

waiting room **machiai-shitsu** 待合室

waitress **jokyū** 女給

Waitress! **Nē-san!** or **Chotto!**

wake up **me ga samemas'** (*sameru, samete*) 目がさめる; (*someone*) **...o okoshimas'** (*okosu, okosh'te*) を起す

walk **arukimas'** (*aruku, aruite*) 歩く; (*takes a*) **sampo shimas'** (*suru, sh'te*) 散歩する

wall (*of house*) **kabe** 壁; (*around courtyard, etc.*) **hei** 塀 「**maguchi** がまぐち

wallet **saifu** 財布 or **satsu-ire** 礼入れ or ga- wander **samayoimas'** (*samayou, samayotte*) さまよう

want (**...ga**) **irimas'** (*iru, itte*) 要る

war **sensō** 戦争

warm **attakai** (*or* **atatakai**) 暖い; (*luke-warm liquids*) **nurui** ぬるい

was *see* is

wash **araimas'** (*arau, aratte*) 洗う; (*laun-der*) **sentaku shimas'** (*suru, sh'te*)洗濯する

washcloth **f'kin** ふきん

washer **sentak'-ki** 洗濯機

washing **sentaku** *or* **sentaku-mono** 洗濯(物)

washroom **o-tearai** お手洗

waste **muda ni shimas'** (*suru, sh'te*) むだに

weigh (... no) **mekata o hakarimas'** (*hakaru, hakatte*) (の)目方を計る

wastebasket (kami)**kuzu-kago** (紙)くずかご

watch **tokei** 時計; *see also* look

water **mizu** 水

waterfall **taki** 滝

watermelon **suika** すいか

water pistol **mizu-deppō** 水鉄砲

waterproof **bōsui** (no) 防水(の)

wave **nami** 波

wax (**mitsu**)**rō** (蜜)蠟 「**yarikata** やりかた

way **michi** 道; (*method*) **sh'kata** 仕方 *or*

(gets in the) way **jama ni narimas'** (*naru, natte*) *or* **jama o shimas'** (*suru, sh'te*) じゃまになる *or* じゃまをする 「退く

(gets out of the) way **dokimas'** (*doku, doite*)

we *see* us

weak **yowai** 弱い

wealthy *see* rich

wear (*on body*) **kimas'** (*kiru, kite*) 着る; (*on legs or feet*) **hakimas'** (*haku, haite*) はく; (*on head*) **kaburimas'** (*kaburu, kabutte*) かぶる; (*on hands*) **hamemas'** (*hameru,*

weather **tenki** 天気 「*hamete*) はめる

weather forecast **tenki-yohō** 天気予報

weave **orimas'** (*oru, otte*) 織る

wedding **kekkon(-sh'ki)** 結婚(式)

Wednesday **suiyōbi** 水曜日

weed **zassō** 雑草

week **shūkan** 週間

weep **nakimas'** (*naku, naite*) 泣く

weight **mekata** 目方 *or* **omosa** 重さ

Welcome! **Yoku irasshaimash'ta!** *or* **Yō**

Welcome home. **O-kaeri nasai.** ⌊**koso!**

(You're) welcome. **Dō itashimash'te.**

well (*for water*) **ido** 井戸

well (*good*) **yoku** よく

were *see* is

west **nishi** 西

wet **nureta** ぬれた

whale **kujira** くじら ⌈*or* n)

what **nani** 何 (*pronounced* **nan** *before* **t, d,**

wheat **komugi** 小麦

wheel **wa** 輪 *or* **sharin** 車輪

when? **itsu** いつ

when......(suru) **to** (する) と *or* ...(**sh'-**)
  tara (し)たら *or* ...(**sh'ta**) **toki** (した)時

where? **doko** 何処

whether ...**ka dō ka** かどうか

which (*of two*) **dochira** どちら *or* **dotchi**
  どっち; (*of more than two*) **dore** どれ

while **aida** 間 ⌈(で打つ)

whip **muchi** (**de uchimas'**; *utsu, utte*) 鞭

whisper **sasayakimas'** (*sasayaku, sasayaite*)
  囁く *or* **mimiuchi shimas'** (*suru, sh'te*)
  耳打する

whistle **fue** 笛; *(with lips)* **kuchi-bue**
  (o f'kimas'; *f'ku, fuite*) 口笛(を吹く)

white **shiroi** 白い

who? **dare** 誰

whole **zentai (no)** 全体(の)

wholesale **oroshi (de)** 卸(で)

whore *see* prostitute

whose **dare no** 誰の

why **dō sh'te** どうして *or* **naze** なぜ

wide **hiroi** 広い

widow **yamome** やもめ *or* **mibōjin** 未亡人

wife **ok'san** 奥さん; *(one's own)* **kanai** 家内

wild *(disorderly)* **rambō (na)** 乱暴(な);
  (rough) **arai** 粗い; *(roughneck)* **abaremono**
  暴れもの; *(not cultivated)* **yama no...**

will *see* shall └山の *or* **yasei no...** 野生の

willow **yanagi** 柳

win **kachimas'** *(katsu, katte)* 勝つ

wind *(breeze)* **kaze** 風

wind (up) **makimas'** *(maku, maite)* 巻く

window **mado** 窓

wine **budō-shu** ぶどう酒

wing *(of bird or plane)* **tsubasa** 翼; *(of insect)* 「**hane** 羽

wink **mabataki** *(shimas'; suru, sh'te)* まば

winter **fuyu** 冬 └たき(する)

wipe **f'kimas'** *(f'ku, fuite)* 拭く

wire **harigane** 針金; *see also* telegram

wise **kash'koi** 賢い

wish for **...ga hoshii** がほしい

123

wish to ... (sh')-tai des' (し)たいです

with ...to と or ...to issho ni と一緒に

without (excluding) ...no hoka ni の外に;
　(not having) ...ga nai to がないと

wolf ōkami おおかみ

woman onna 女

(I) wonder ... ... ka shira. かしら

wonderful subarashii すばらしい or s'teki
　(na) すてき(な)

wood ki 木 or mokuzai 木材

wood-block print mokuhanga 木版画

wooden shoes geta 下駄

woods see forest

wool yōmo 羊毛 or keito 毛糸

word kotoba ことば or tango 単語

work hatarakimas' (hataraku, hataraite)
　働く or shigoto (o shimas'; suru, sh'te)
　仕事(をする)

worker shokkō 職工 or rōdōsha 労働者

world sekai 世界

worm mushi 虫

worry shimpai (shimas'; suru, sh'te) 心配

worse motto warui もっと悪い

worst ichiban warui 一ばん悪い

worth see value

would see perhaps

wrap tsutsumimas' (tsutsumu, tsutsunde)
　　　　　　　　　　　　　　　　　「包む

wreck (car) jiko 事故 or shōtotsu 衝突

wrestling resuringu レスリング; (profes-

sional) **puro-resu** ブロ・レス; (*Japanese*

wrinkle **shiwa** しわ ⌊*style*) **sumō** すもう

write **kakimas'** (*kaku, kaite*) 書く

wrong (*mistaken*) **machigatta** 間違つた

Y

yard **niwa** 庭 ⌈をする

yawn **akubi o shimas'** (*suru, sh'te*) あくび

year **toshi** *or* **-nen** 年

yell *see* shout

yellow **kiiroi** 黄色い

yes **hai** はい *or* **ē** ええ

yesterday **kinō** 昨日

yet **mada** まだ

you **anta** あんた *or* **anata** あなた ⌈たたち

you all **mina san** 皆さん *or* **anta-tachi** あん

young **wakai** 若い

your(s) **anta no** あんたの

youth (*young man*) **seinen** 青年

Z

zero **rei** 零; (*written symbol*) **maru** 0

zipper **chakku** チャック *or* **jippā** ジッパー

zone **chitai** 地帯 *or* **kuiki** 区域

zoo **dōbutsuen** 動物園

125

PART II

Japanese-English

NOTE: Verbs are given in both the polite present (**-mas'**) and the plain present (**-u**). Where these two forms would be at about the same place in alphabetical order, they are given together; when they are rather different in shape, you will find two entries. Occasionally a word is out of alphabetical order for convenience, but not more than a place or two. If you do not find the word you are looking for, glance up and down the page a bit. Note that **f'** is alphabetized as **fu**, **ts'** as **tsu**, **s'** as **su**, etc.; **sh'** is alphabetized as **shi**, and **ch'** as **chi**.

A

abekku a couple (on a date), a date
abunai dangerous
abura oil, fat, grease
agarimas', agaru goes up
agemas', ageru raises up; gives
aida interval; between; while
aimas' (au) meets; sees (a person)
ainiku unfortunately
aisatsu greeting
aite the other fellow (companion; adversary)
aitsu that one over there
ajā, ajappā well, I'll be...!
aji taste
aka-chan baby
akai red
akabō redcap
akambō baby
akarui bright, light
akemas', akeru opens; leaves empty
aki autumn, fall
akimas', aku is open; is empty
amai sweet
ame¹ rain
ame² candy
ami net
ammari too much, overly

ana hole
anata you
ane older sister
ani older brother
ano that (over there) ⌈(one's anxieties)
anshin shimas' (**suru**) doesn't worry, relaxes
anta you
aoi blue ; green
arai rough, coarse
araimas', **arau** washes ⌈corrects
aratamemas', **aratameru** changes, alters,
arawaremas', **arawareru** appears, shows
are that one (over there) ⌊up, comes out
ari ant
arigato (**gozaimas'**) thank you
arimas', **aru** there is ; we've got
arimash'ta there was ; we had
aru a certain
arubaito a side job, a sideline
arui-wa or else, maybe
arukimas', **aruku** walks
asa morning
asai shallow
ase sweat
ashi foot ; leg
asobi fun ; a game ; a visit
asobimas', **asobu** has fun ; plays ; visits
asoko, **as'ko** (that place) over there
atama head

atarashii new

atarimas'. ataru hits, faces; applies; is

at(a)takai warm ⌐correct

atemas', ateru guesses; hits; sets aside, appropriates, designates; touches; ad-

atena address ⌐dresses

ato after(wards), later

atsui[1] hot

atsui[2] thick

atsumarimas', atsumaru meet, assemble

atsumemas', atsumeru collects, gathers

au (aimas') meets, sees (a person)

awasemas', awaseru puts together, combines

azarashi seal (*animal*)

azukemas', azukeru entrusts, checks, deposits

B

-ba place

baai, bawai situation, case, circumstance

bai double

baka fool, idiot, stupid

ban[1] guard, watch; number

ban[2] evening

basho place

basu 1. bus 2. bath

batā butter

Beikoku America

beni rouge
benjo toilet
benkyō study
benri handy, convenient
bentō (box) lunch
betsu separate, special, particular
bin bottle ; jar
bōi boy, waiter, steward, clerk
boku I, me (man speaking)
bokushi minister, pastor ; Reverend
bōshi hat
botan button
bōzu Buddhist monk or priest
bu part, division, section
budō grapes
budō-shu wine
bumpō grammar
bun part, portion, share ; state, status
bungo literary language
bunka culture
bunshō (written) sentence
buta pig
buta-niku pork
byōin hospital
byōki sick ; sickness

C

cha tea

chadai tip

chakku zipper

champon alternating. skipping back and forth, mixing one's drinks (as beer and chi blood ⌊saké)

chi blood ⌊saké)

chichi[1] father

chichi[2] breasts; mother's milk

chigaimas', chigau is different; is wrong; is

chihō area, region ⌊isn't like that

chiisai. chiisa-na little. small

chiizu cheese

chika subway; underground; basement

chikai near, close by

chika-michi short cut

chikki[1] check, receipt, stub

chikki[2] stick hair-grease

chikuonki phonograph

chippu tip

chiri geography

chiri-gami Japanese Kleenex and toilet paper

chizu map

chō[1] block of a city

chō[2] head, chief, leader

chōdai please; I (humbly) take

chokki vest

chokusetsu direct

chō-kyori long distance

chōsa examination, investigation, inquiry

Chōsen Korea

chotto just a little ; just a minute

chū middle , medium

chūgakkō middle school (junior high school)

chūgata medium-size (model)

Chūgoku China

chūi[1] attention

chūi[2] 1st lieutenant ; lieutenant j. g.

chūshin center

D

da (des') is ; it is

da ga but

dai- big

dai-(ichi) number (one)

daiben bowel movement

daigaku college, university

daiji important, precious

daijōbu OK, all right ; safe and sound ; no need to worry

daiku carpenter

daitai in general, on the whole, approximately, almost

da kara (sa) and so ; therefore ; that's why

dakimas', daku holds in the arms

damarimas', damaru is silent ; shuts up

damashimas', damasu deceives

dambō heating (in a house)

dame no good, no use, won't do ; don't !

dandan gradually

danna (san) master of the house ; husband

dantai organization, group

dare who

dare ka somebody

dare mo everybody ; nobody

dashi soup-stock ⌈mails ; begins

dashimas', dasu puts out ; produces ; spends ;

da tte but ⌈of)

de[1] (happening) at, in, on ; with, by (means

de[2] is and ; being, its being ; with (its being)

de gozaimas' = de

deguchi exit

dekigoto happening, accident

dekimas', dekiru can, is possible ; is pro-
 duced ; is finished, ready

dekimono swelling, sore, boil, pimple

demas', deru goes out, comes out, leaves,

dembu buttocks, hips ⌊starts

de mo but, however, even so

dempō telegram

denki electricity ; lights

densha electric car (streetcar or elevated)

dentō 1. lamp, light, flashlight 2. tradition,
 convention

denwa telephone (call)

depāto department store ⌈starts

deru (demas') goes out, comes out, leaves,

desh'ta was ; it was

deshō probably, probably is, it probably is

des', da is; it is; it is a case of . . .

de wa (= ja) well then; in that case; and so ; and now

dō how, why ; (in) what (way)

doa door

dochira which one

dochira ka either one of the two

dochira mo either one ; neither one ; both

Doitsu Germany

doitsu which one

dokimas' (doku) gets out of the way

doko where

doko ka somewhere

doko mo everywhere ; nowhere

doku[1] poison

doku[2] **(dokimas')** gets out of the way

donna what kind of

dōmo 1. thank you 2. excuse me 3. ever

dono which

dore which one

doro mud

dorobō thief, robber

doru dollar

dō-sh'te why ; how

dotchi = dochira

dotera padded bathrobe

doyōbi Saturday

dōzo please

E

e picture
ē yes
ebi shrimp; lobster
eda branch
e-hagaki picture postcard
e-hon picture book
eiga (-kan) movie (theater)
Eigo English
Eikoku England
eisei hygiene, health, sanitation
eki railroad station
en Yen
empitsu pencil
enkai party
ensoku picnic, outing
entotsu chimney, smokestack
erabimas', erabu chooses, selects, elects
erai great, superior

F

fu an urban prefecture (Kyoto or Osaka)
fū appearance, air; way, fashion, manner
fuben inconvenient, unhandy
fuchūi carelessness
fuda label, tag, card, check

fude writing brush

fudōsan real estate

fūfu husband and wife, Mr. and Mrs.

fuhei discontent, grumbling

fuhō illegal

fui suddenly

fujin lady

fu-jiyū inconvenient : needy : weak

fukai, f'kai deep

fukimas', f'kimas' see fuku, f'ku

fukin, f'kin napkin, towel, cloth

fuku, f'ku[1] 1. blows 2. wipes

fuku. f'ku[2] clothes, suit, dress

fukuro, f'kuro bag, sack

fukushū, f'kushū review

fukuzatsu, f'kuzatsu complicated

fuman discontented. dissatisfied

fumei unknown, obscure

fumimas', fumu steps on

fun minute

funayoi seasick(ness)

fundoshi a loincloth, a jockstrap

fune boat

fun-iki atmosphere

Furansu France

furemas', fureru touches, comes in contact [with

furi manner, air, pretense

furimas', furu[1] precipitates (rains, snows)

furimas', furu[2] waves, shakes, wags

138

furo bath

furōnin vagabond, tramp

furoshiki, furosh'ki a cloth wrapper

furu second-hand

furui old

furyō bad, no good

fūryū elegant

fusagimas', fusagu stops up, closes, blocks

fusawasnii suitable, worthy ; becoming

fusegimas', fusegu prevents ; defends, protects

fushigi strange ; wonderful ; suspicious

fusoku shortage, deficiency, scarcity

fusuma opaque sliding door

futa, f'ta lid

futari, f'tari two persons

futatsu, f'tatsu two; two years old; 2nd day

futo, f'to unexpectedly

futoi, f'toi fat, plump

futon, f'ton Japanese padded quilt

futsuka two days

fuyu winter

G

ga[1] SUBJECT PARTICLE (*shows the actor :* who ⌊does, what is)

ga[2] but ; and

gai damage, harm, injury ⌈pean)

gaijin foreigner (usually American or Euro-

gaikō-kan diplomat

gaikoku abroad ; foreign countries

Gaimu-shō Ministry of Foreign Affairs

gakkō school

gaku learning, study, science

gakumon knowledge, learning, education

gakusei, gak'sei student, schoolboy

gakusha, gak'sha scholar

gamaguchi purse, pocketbook, wallet

gaman shimas' is patient, puts up with

gaman dekimasen (dekinai) can't stand it

gan-yaku a pill

garasu glass

gasorin gasoline

gasorin-sutando (-s'tando) filling station

gasu, gas' gas

gasu-dai gas bill

gehin vulgar

gei arts, accomplishments ; tricks, stunts

geijutsu art(s)

geisha a geisha girl

geki play, drama

gekijō theater

gekkyū monthly salary

gemmai unpolished rice

gemmitsu strict

gendai modern, up-to-date

gengo language

gen-in cause, origin, root

140

genki in good spirits, healthy, cheerful, vigorous

genkin, gen-nama cash, ready money

genshi(-bakudan) atom (bomb)

genzai the present (time)

genzō shimas' develops (film)

geppu monthly instalments

geri diarrhea

geri-dome anti-diarrhetic, paregoric

geshuku lodgings ; board and room

-getsu month

getsuyōbi Monday

gikai the Japanese Diet (Congress)

gimon question, doubt

gimu duty, obligation

gin silver

ginkō bank

giri obligation, sense of obligation, honor

go 1. five 2. checkers

-go language

gofuku-ya dry goods store

gogatsu May

gogo P.M., afternoon

gohan cooked rice: meal; food

go-jū fifty

Gokigen yō! 1. Goodbye 2. Hello

goku very, exceedingly

Gomen kudasai! Hello—anybody home ?

Gomen nasai. Excuse me.

141

gomi trash, rubbish, dust

gomu rubber

goran... (you) look, see, try

Goshimpai naku! Don't worry about it.

go-yō your business

gozaimas' = arimas'

guai condition, shape, feelings (of health)

gumpuku military uniform

gun army, troops

gunjin soldier, military man

gunsō sergeant

guntai troops, army

gunzoku civilian attached to the army,

gutai-teki concrete, substantial, tangible,

gūzen accidentally ⌐material

gyaku opposite, contrary

gyofu fisherman

gyōgi behavior, manners

gyūniku beef

gyūnyū milk

H

ha tooth

haba width

habukimas', **habuku** cuts out, reduces,

hachi¹ eight ⌐saves, eliminates, omits

hachi² bowl, basin

hachi³ (mitsu-bachi) bee

hachi-jū eighty

hadaka naked

hadashi barefoot

hae housefly

hagaki postcard

hage bald

hageshii violent, severe

haha mother

hai[1] yes

hai[2] ashes

hai[3] cupful

haibyō TB

hai-iro gray

haikara fashionable, high-class

hairimas', hairu enters; is inside

haitte imas' is inside

haitatsu delivery

haiyū actor

hajimarimas', hajimaru it begins (starts)

hajime the beginning; in the beginning

hajimete for the first time

hajimemas', hajimeru begins (starts) it

Hajimemash'te. How do you do. (on being introduced)

hakari measuring scales

hakarimas', hakaru measures, weighs

hakimas' (haku) 1. vomits, spits out 2. sweeps 3. wears on feet

hakkiri plainly, clearly, distinctly

143

hakkō publication

hako box

hakobimas', hakobu carries, conveys

haku 1. vomits, spits out 2. sweeps 3. wears ⌊on feet

hama beach

hambun half

hamemas', hameru wears (on fingers)

ha-migaki dentifrice, toothpaste, tooth-han¹ half ⌊powder

han² a seal (to stamp one's name with)

hana¹ flower

hana² nose

hanabi fireworks

hanagata a star (in a theatrical production)

hanao thong (on geta) ⌈distant

hanaremas', hanareru separates, becomes

hanashi talk, story, tale

hanashimas', hanasu speaks, talks; lets loose, lets go, sets free

hane feather; wing

han-i scope, range

hantai opposite, contrary, reverse

hantō peninsula

happa leaf

hara¹ belly, stomach

hara² field ⌈shakes out

haraimas', harau 1. pays 2. brushes aside,

haremas', hareru 1. (weather) clears up

hari needle; hand (of clock) ⌊2. swells up

144

harimas', haru sticks on, pastes; spreads, stretches

haru springtime

hasami scissors, clippers

hashi[1] bridge

hashi[2] (o-hashi) chopsticks

hashigo ladder, stairs

hashirimas', hashiru runs

hasu oblique, slanting

hata flag

hatake field

hataki duster

hatakimas', hataku slap, beat; dust

hatarakimas', hataraku works

hato pigeon, dove

hatoba pier, wharf

hatsumei invention

hatsuon pronunciation

hattatsu development

hayai, hayaku fast, quick

hayarimas', hayaru is popular, is in fashion

hayashi[1] forest

hayashi[2] hash

hazu is expected to; is supposed to; is reasonable to expect

hazukashii ashamed

hazumimas'. hazumu bounces back; cheers

hazuremas', hazureru gets disconnected, comes off, misses, fails

hazushimas', hazusu disconnects, takes off, leaves one's seat

he flatulence

hebi snake ⌐tranged
hedatarimas', hedataru is distant, is es-
hedatemas', hedateru separates them, es-
hedo vomit ⌊tranges them, gets them apart
hei wall, fence
heiki calm, composed, cool, ındifferent
heikin average
heitai soldier
heiwa peace
heizei usually, ordinarily, generally
hekomimas', hekomu gets hollow, depressed
hema bungle, mess
hen[1] (**na**) strange, odd, queer
hen[2] vicinity, neighborhood
henji answer
henka change ⌐down, shortens, curtails
herashimas', he-rasu decreases, cuts it
heri border, edge ⌐dles
herimas', herıı goes down, decreases, dwin-
heso navel, bellybutton
heta unskilful, poor, inexpert
heya room
hi[1] fire
hi[2] 1. day 2. sun
hibachi charcoal brazier
hibikimas', hibiku echoes, resounds
hidari left
hidoi severe, unreasonable, terrible
hidoku hard, cruelly, terribly

146

hiemas', hieru gets cold
higashi east
hige beard, mustache
higeki tragedy
hiji elbow
hijō emergency
hijō ni extremely
hikaku comparison
hikarimas', hikaru shines ⌈and")
hiki- VERB PREFIX ("pull and" or "take
hikidashi drawer
hiki-kaemasu, -kaeru exchanges, converts
hikimas' (hiku) pulls (out); draws; drags; catches; attracts; subtracts; deducts; looks up a word ⌈dence)
hikkoshimas', hikkosu moves (one's resi-
hikōjō airport
hikōki airplane
hikō-yūbin airmail
hikui low, short
hima time; leisure, spare time; furlough, leave; dismissal (of servant); slow (busi-
himitsu secret, mystery ⌊ness)
himo string, cord, tape, strap
hin quality; elegance, refinement, dignity
hinan blame, censure, reproach
hinerimas', hineru twists
hiniku sarcasm; sarcastic; cynical
hinshitsu quality

147

hi-oi awning, sunshade, blind ⌈takes
hipparimas', hipparu pulls, drags, tugs at,
hiragana the roundish Japanese letters
hirakimas'. hiraku opens up
hirattai flat
Hirippin Philippines
hiroba a square, a plaza, an open space
hiroi wide, broad
hiroimas', hirou picks up
hiru daytime; noon
hiru kara afternoon
hiru-ma daytime
hisashi-buri ni after a long time (of absence)
hitai forehead, brow
hitei shimas' denies
hito person, man
hito- one
hitori one person
hitoshii equal, identical, similar
hitotsu one; one year old; one and the same
hitsuji sheep
hitsuyō necessity, need; necessary
hiya (o-hiya) cold water
hiyashimas', hiyasu cools it off; refrigerates
hiyō cost, expense
hiyori weather; conditions
hiza knee, lap
hizuke date
hō¹ alternative; one (of two); direction, way

148

hō² law; rule; method

hōbi (go-hōbi) prize, reward

hōbō everywhere, all over, every which way

hodo extent; limits; moderation; approximate time; (not) so much as; the more...

hodokimas', hodoku undoes, unties

hoka other, in addition to, other than

hoken insurance

hokkyoku North Pole, Arctic

hokori¹ pride, boast

hokori² dust

hoku- north-

hōkyū pay, salary

hombu central office

hōmen direction, quarter, district

homemas', homeru praises

hommono the real thing

hōmon call, visit

hon book

hon- main; chief; this; the; present

hondō the main route

hone bone

honki serious, earnest

honno a slight, just a little, a mere

honrai originally, from the start

hontō, honto true; truth; really

hon-yaku translation

hoppeta cheek

hoppō north

149

Hora ! Huh ?! What's that ?! Look at that !

hora[1] cave

hora[2] trumpet-shell; exaggerration

horemas', horeru falls in love, takes a fancy [to

hori ditch, moat

horidashi-mono a bargain, a real find

hōritsu law

horiwari canal

horimas', horu digs, excavates

hoshi star

hoshi-(gaki) dried (persimmons)

hoshii is desired ; desires, wants

hoshimas', hosu dries it

hoshō guarantee

hōsō (-kyoku) broadcast (station)

hosoi slender

hosu (hoshimas') dries it

hōtai bandage

hoteru hotel

Hotoke-sama Buddha

hotondo almost (all); almost all the time

hyaku hundred

hyaku-man million

hyakushō farmer

hyō table, schedule

hyōban reputation, fame

hyōgen expression (words)

hyōgu-ya paper-hanger, paper repairman

hyōjō expression (on face)

hyōjun standard
hyōjun-go standard Japanese
hyōmen surface
hyotto accidentally, by chance
hyotto sh'tara maybe, possibly
hyūzu fuse

I

i- medicine, doctoring
ian consolation; recreation
ichi[1] one
ichi[2] (**ichi-ba**) market, marketplace
ichi[3] position
ichiban number one; first; best; most
ichibu a part, portion
ichido one time
ichijirushii conspicuous, prominent, striking
ichijitsu one day; some day
ichimai a sheet; one
ido a well
ie a house
igai unexpected
igaku medicine, medical studies
... igo afterwards, from ... on
ii good
ii(-) (infinitive of **yū** "saying")
iie no
iimas', yū says

151

iimash'ta said
iin committee (member)
iin-kai committee
ii-wake explanation, excuse
iji temper, disposition
... ijō above, upwards of ...
ijō unusual
... ika below, less than ...
ika medical department
ikada raft
ikaga how (about it)?
ikagawashii suspicious, questionable, shady
ikari anger
ike pond
ikebana flower arrangement ⌈don't
ikemasen, ikenai it won't do; you mustn't;
iken opinion
iki breath
iki (na) smart, stylish
iki(-) (infinitive of **iku** " going")
ikioi vigor, energy, spirit
ikimas', iku goes
ikiru (ikite imas') lives, is alive
ik-ko one (piece)
iku (ikimas') goes
ikura how much
ikutsu how many; how old
ima now
imas', iru is, stays

152

imi meaning
imo potato
imōto younger sister
in seal, stamp
inai within
inaka country
inchiki fake, fraud
Indo India
Indoneshiya Indonesia
ine rice-plant
infure inflation
inki ink
inki (na) gloomy
inochi one's life
inori prayer
inshō impression
interi intellectual; highbrow
inu dog
ippai 1. full 2. a cupful (glassful)
...irai since ...
Irasshai(mase)! Welcome!
irasshaimas', irassharu (someone honored)
　　1. comes; 2. goes; 3. stays, is
ireba false teeth
iremas', ireru puts in, lets in
iriguchi entrance
irimas', iru¹ 1. is necessary; needs; wants
iru² (imas') is, stays ⌊2. roasts 3. shoots
iro color; sex

isha doctor, physician

ishi[1] stone

ishi[2] will, intention

isogashii busy

isogimas', isogu hurries, rushes

issai all, everything, without exception

issaku-ban(-jitsu) night (day) before last

issho (ni) together with

isshō one's whole life

isshō-kemmei desperately; very hard

isshu a kind, a sort

isu chair

ita board, plank

itai painful, hurting

itami an ache, a pain

itashimas', itasu I (humbly) do

itazura mischief, prank

itchi agreement

ito thread, yarn; silk

itoko cousin

itoma =hima

itsu when

itsu-ka 1. 5 days; 5th day 2. sometime

itsutsu five

itsuwari falsehood, lie

ittai ...on earth, ...indeed

itte 1. going, goes and (gerund of **iku**) 2.
=**yutte**: saying, says and (gerund of **yū**)

ittei fixed, settled, definite

ittō first, first class
iwa rock, crag
iwai celebration, party
iwayuru so-called, what you might call
iya no
iya (na) unpleasant; disagreeable; disliked
iyashii lowly, vulgar
iyo-iyo 1. at last 2. in fact 3. more and more
izen since, before, ago

J

ja, jā well, well then; in that case; now
ja arimasen (ja nai) it is not; it is not a case of
jagaimo Irish potatoes
jama interference, disturbance, hindrance, obstacle
jari gravel, pebbles
ji[1] a letter; a Chinese character
ji[2] hemorrhoids
ji[3] land, ground; texture; fabric
-ji o'clock
jibiki dictionary
jibun oneself; myself; alone
jidai age, period, era, time
jidōsha automobile
jidō-teki automatic
jigyō enterprise, business
jihen incident, happening
jijō circumstances; conditions

155

jikan time ; hour
jika ni directly ; personally
jiki ni immediately ; soon
jikken experiment
jikkō performance ; practice ; realization
jiko accident
jiku axis, axle
jiman pride, boast
jimi plain, sober
jimu business, office work
jimuin office clerk
jimusho office
-jin person
jinkō population
jisatsu suicide
jishin¹ earthquake
jishin² self-confidence
jissai actual conditions, reality ; in practice ; ⌈in fact, really
jitensha bicycle
jitsu truth ; truly, really
jitsugyō business
jitsugyō-ka businessman
jitsuyō practical use, utility
jiyū freedom, free ; fluent, at ease
jōbu healthy, sturdy
jochū maid-servant
jōdan joke
jokyū waitress
jōriku disembarking, landing

jorō(-ya) whore(-house)

jōsha getting into a car, boarding

... joshi Madame, Miss, Mrs.

jōshiki common sense

jōtai condition, situation, circumstances

jōtō the best, first-rate

jōzu skilled, clever, good at

jū¹ ten

jū² gun

-jū throughout the...

jūbako nestling boxes, Chinese boxes

jūbun enough

jūdō jujitsu

jū-hachi eighteen

jū-ichi eleven

jūji a cross

jūku nineteen

jukugo a compound word

jū-man a hundred thousand

jumbi preparations

jun order, turn

jun (na) pure

jū-ni twelve ⌜is made to accord with

jun-jimas', -jiru applies correspondingly;

junjo order

junkan circulation; cycle

junsa policeman

jū-roku sixteen

jūsho residence

157

jūsu 1. orange soda pop 2. juice
jūtan rug, carpet
jūyō important
juzu beads

K

ka mosquito
...ka ? QUESTION PARTICLE
...ka some ...., any ...
...ka... ... or ...
kabe wall
kabin flower vase
kabu stock (in a company)
kabushiki kaisha a corporation
kaburimas', kaburu wears on head
kachimas', katsu wins
kado (outside) corner
kaemas', kaeru[1] changes, exchanges
kaerimas', kaeru[2] goes home, goes back
kaeru[3] frog
kaeshimas', kaesu returns it
kaette contrary to expectations
kagaku science
kagami mirror
kage shade
kage-bōshi shadow
kagi key
kagimas', kagu smells it

kagiri limit, extent

kago basket

kagu furniture

kagu (kagimas') smells it

kai a meeting

-kai times, occasions

kaichū one's pocket

kaidan steps, stairs

kaidō an auditorium

kaigai overseas, abroad

kaigan seashore

kaigi meeting, conference

kaigun navy

kaii itchy

kaikan a public hall, a building

kaikei accounts

kaimas', kau¹ buys

kaimas', kau² raises, keeps (animals)

kaimono shopping

kaisha company

kaiwa conversation

kaji a fire

kajirimas', kajiru gnaws, nibbles

kakarimas', kakaru 1. it hangs 2. it takes, it requires 3. begins

kake 1. gambling; a bet 2. credit

kakemas', kakeru¹ 1. hangs it 2. telephones

kakemas', kakeru² bets

kakemas', kakeru³ runs, gallops

kakemas', kakeru multiplies

kaki[1] persimmon

kaki[2] oyster

kakimas', kaku writes; scratches

kakitome registered mail

kakomimas', kakomu surrounds

kaku writes; scratches

kakuremas', kakureru it hides

kakushimas', kakusu hides it

kama 1. pot; boiler 2. stove, oven, kiln 3. sickle

kamado kitchen range, stove

kamaimasen it makes no difference

kamban signboard

kami[1] hair (on the head)

kami[2] paper

kami-sama God; gods

kaminari thunder

kamisori razor

kamits'kimas', kamits'ku bites

kamo 1. wild duck 2. sucker, dupe

...ka mo shiremasen maybe ...

kampai a toast, "bottoms up"

kampan deck

kan a can

-kan for the interval of

kana Japanese syllabic writing

kanai my wife

kanamono hardware

kanarazu for sure

kanari fairly, rather

кanashii sad

kane money ; metal ; bell

kangae thought, idea. opinion

kangaemas', kangaeru thinks

kangofu nurse

kani crab

kanji[1] feeling

kanji[2] a Chinese character (letter)

kanjimas', kanjiru feels

kanjō bill ⌜concern

kankei connection, relationship. interest,

kan-kiri can opener

kankō sightseeing

kankōkyaku tourist

kanōsei possibility

kansha thanks, gratitude

kanshin[1] concern, interest

kanshin[2] **shimas'** admires

kanshō interference, meddling

kantan simple

kanzei customs duty

kanzen perfect

kanzō liver

kao face ; looks, a look ⌜shoplifts

kapparaimas', kapparau swipes, steals,

kara[1] shell, crust

kara[2] empty

161

...**kara** from ; since ; because, so

karada body

karai 1. spicy, hot, peppery 2. salty

karashi mustard

karasu crow

kare he, him

kare-ra they, them

kare-shi lover, paramour ; boy friend ; husband

karē-raisu rice curry

kari temporary

karimas', kariru borrows

karimas', karu cuts, mows

karui light (of weight)

kasa umbrella

kasanarimas', kasanaru they pile up

kasanemas', kasaneru piles them up, puts one on top of another

kasegimas', kasegu earns, works for (money)

kashi (o-kashi) cakes, sweets, pastry

kashima rooms for rent

kashimas' kasu lends

...**ka shira** I wonder if...

kashiya house for rent

kasu sédiment, dregs

kasu (kashimas') lends

kasumi haze, mist

kata[1] shoulder

kata[2] form, shape, size, mold, pattern

kata[3] person, honored person

-kata manner of doing, way

katachi form, shape

katagi respectable, steady, honest

katahō, kattappō one of a pair; the other one (of a pair)

katai hard; strong; upright; strict

katakana the squarish Japanese letters

katamari a lump

katamukimas', katamuku leans

katana sword

katarimas', kataru relates, tells

katawa cripple

katazukemas', katazukeru puts in order, straightens up, cleans up

katei[1] home, household, family

katei[2] hypothesis, supposition

katsu (kachimas') wins

katsu a Japanese "cutlet"; anything fried in deep fat

katsudō action, activity, movement, liveliness

katsugimas', katsugu carries on shoulders

katsuo (-bushi) a (dried) bonito fish

katsura a wig

katte[1] kitchen

katte[2] **(ni)** selfish(ly), as one wants to

kau[1] **(kaimas')** buys

kau[2] **(kaimas')** raises, keeps (animals)

kawa[1] river

kawa[2] skin

kawaii, kawairashii cute, loveable, darling

kawai-sō pitiful

kawakimas', kawaku gets dry

kawara tile

kawari change, substitute

kawarimas' kawaru it changes; it takes

kawase a money order ⌊the place of

kaya mosquito net

kayōbi Tuesday

kayoimas'. kayou commutes, goes back and forth, goes (regularly)

kayu rice-gruel, porridge

kayui itchy

kazan volcano

kazari (-mono) ornament, decoration

kazarimas', kazaru decorates

kaze 1. wind 2. a cold

kazoemas', kazoeru counts

kazoku family

kazu number

ke hair, wool, feathers

kechim-bo stingy person, skinflint

kedo = keredo(mo)

kega wound, injury

keiba horse racing

keiba-jō a racetrack

keibetsu despise

keiei management, operation

keikaku plan, scheme

164

keiken experience

kieki business conditions, prosperity, boom

keiko exercise, practice, drill

keirin bicycle race

keisan calculation, computation

keisatsu police

keishiki form, formality

keiyaku contract, agreement

keizai economics, finances

kēki a cake

kekka result; as a result (consequence)

kekkō 1. splendid; excellent 2. fairly well, well enough; enough

Kekkō des'. No, thank you.

kekkon marriage

kekkyoku after all, in the long run

kembutsu sightseeing

kempei MP; shore patrol

kempō constitution

kemuri smoke

ken a Japanese prefecture (like a state)

kenchiku construction; architecture

kencho the prefectural government (office)

kenka quarrel

kenkō health

kenkyū research, study ⌈check-up

kensa, kensatsu inspection, examination,

ken-yaku economy, thrift, economizing

ke-orimono woolen goods

165

keredo(mo) however, though, but
kerimas', keru kicks
keshiki scenery, view
keshimas', kesu puts out; turns off; erases
keshō cosmetics, make-up
keshō-shitsu ladies lounge
kessan settling accounts
kesseki absent
kesshin determination, resolution
kesu (keshimas') puts out; turns off; erases
kettei determination, decision
ketten flaw, defect
ki[1] spirit; feeling; mind, heart
ki[2] tree; wood
kibishii strict, severe
kibō hope
kibun feeling, mood
kichi military base
ki-chigai mad, insane
kichin-to punctual; precise; neat
kido entrance gate, wicket
kiemas', kieru is extinguished, goes out; ⌊fades, vanishes
ki-iro yellow
ki-ito raw silk
kiji[1] article, news item
kiji[2] pheasant
kikai[1] chance, opportunity
kikai[2] machine, machinery
kikan engine; instrument; agency

kikasemas', kikaseru lets someone hear, tells, informs
kiken danger, peril
kiki-me ga arimas' is effective
kikimas', kiku listens, hears; obeys; asks; is effective, works
kikō climate
kikoemas', kikoeru can be heard, can hear
kiku (kikimas') listens, hears; obeys; asks; is effective, works
kiku chrysanthemum
kimarimas', kimaru is settled, is arranged
kimas'¹, kuru comes
kimas²', kiru wears
kimben industrious, hardworking
kime grain, texture
kimemas', kimeru settles, arranges
kimi¹ you
kimi² feeling, sensation
kim-makie gold lacquer
kimo liver
kimochi feeling, sensation
kimono clothes; a kimono
kimpatsu blond
kimyō strange, peculiar
kin gold
kina quinine
kinen commemoration
kinem-bi anniversary
Kin-en No Smoking
kingyo goldfish
kinjo neighborhood, vicinity

167

kinō yesterday

ki-no-doku pitiful, pitiable

kinoko mushrooms

kinshi prohibition, ban

kinu silk

kin-yōbi Friday

kin-yū finance

kinzoku metal

kioku memory

kippu ticket

kirai is disliked ; dislikes

kire a piece, a cut

kirei pretty ; clean   ⌈3. breaks down

kiremas', **kireru** 1. cuts (well) 2. runs out

kireme a gap, a break, a pause

kiri¹ fog, mist

kiri² a hole-punch, an awl, a drill

kiri³ paulownia (tree or wood)

...(k)kiri only, just

kirimas', **kiru** cuts

kiritsu discipline   ⌈4. kiloliter

kiro 1. kilogram 2. kilometer 3. kilowatt

kiroku record

kiru¹ (**kirimas'**) cuts

kiru² (**kimas'**) puts on, wears

kiryō personal appearance, looks ; ability

kisen steamship

kisetsu season

kisha¹ railroad train

kisha[2] newspaperman, reporter

kishi shore, coast, bank

kishukusha dormitory, boarding house

kisoku rule, regulation

kissa-ten a tearoom

kita[1] north

kita[2] came (past tense of **kuru**); wore (past tense of **kiru**)

kitanai dirty

kite coming, comes and (gerund of **kuru**); wearing, wears and (gerund of **kiru**)

kitsui 1. tight 2. severe 3. bold

kitsune fox

kitte stamp

kitto no doubt, surely

kiwa brink, edge

kiwadoi dangerous, delicate, ticklish

kiwamarimas', kiwamaru comes to an end; gets carried to extremes

kiwamemas', kiwameru carries to extremes; investigates thoroughly

kiwamete extremely

kizamimas'. kizamu chops fine; carves; notches, nicks

kizashi symptoms, signs, indications

kizu wound; crack, flaw; fault, defect

kizu-ato scar

ko child; person

kō[1] this way, so, like this

kō[2] incense

kōba factory

kobamimas', kobamu refuses, rejects ; opposes, resists

kōban police box

koboshimas', kobosu spills

kobu bump, knob, swelling

kobun henchman, subordinate, follower

kobune small boat

kobushi fist

kōcha black tea

kochira 1. here, this way 2. this one 3. me, I ; us, we

kodai ancient times

kōdō[1] highway

kōdō[2] action, behavior

kodomo child ; boy

koe voice ; cry

kōen[1] public park

kōen[2] lecture

kōen[3] support

kōfu workman

kōfuku happiness

kōfun excitement

kōgai suburbs

kogashimas', kogasu scorches

kogata small-size (model)

kōgeki attack

kōgi lecture

kogimas', kogu rows

kogitte check

kōgo spoken language, colloquial

Kōgō sama the Empress

kogoe low voice, whisper

kogoto scolding

kogu (kogimas') rows

kōgyō industry

kōhei fair, impartial

kōhii coffee ; **-ten, -ya** coffeeshop

koi[1] carp (fish)

koi[2] love

koi[3] request

kōi goodwill

koibito sweetheart

koitsu this one

kōji construction work

kojiki beggar

kojin individual

kōjitsu excuse, pretext

kōkai public

kōkan exchange

koke moss

kōkishin curiosity, inquisitiveness

kokkai assembly, parliament, congress, Diet

kokkei amusing, funny

kokku cook

koko here, this place

kokonotsu nine

kokonoka 9 days ; the 9th day

kōkoku advertisement

kokoro mind, heart, spirit, feeling

kokoro-mochi feelings, spirit, mood

171

kokorozuke tip, gratuity
kokuban blackboard
kokubō national defense ⌜elevated)
Kokuden Government Electric (the Tokyo
Kokujin Negro
kokumin a people, a nation
kokunai internal, domestic, inland
kokuritsu national, government-run
kokusai international
kokuseki nationality
kokyō hometown, birthplace
kokyū respiration, breathing
koma a toy top
komakai 1. fine, small 2. detailed, exact
  3. thrifty 4. small change
komarimas', komaru gets perplexed, embar-
komban tonight ⌊rassed, is at a loss
Komban wa. Good evening.
kombō club, billy-club, bludgeon
kombu (kind of seaweed)
kome rice
komi-itta complicated, intricate, elaborate
komori babysitter
kōmori 1. bat 2. umbrella
kompon foundation, basis ⌜curs
kōmurimas', kōmuru sustains, suffers, in-
kon dark blue
kona powder; flour
kona-gusuri powdered medicine

konashimas', konasu powders; digests

kondo this time ; next time

kongetsu this month

kongo from now on, in the future

konkūru prize contest

konna such a

konnan difficulty, trouble, hardship

Konnichi wa. Good afternoon. (Hello.)

kono this

kono-aida lately   ⌈fers

konomimas', konomu likes, is fond of, pre-

kon-yaku engagement (to be married)

konzatsu confusion, jumble, disorder

koppu a glass, a cup

koraemas', koraeru 1. stands, bears 2. con-

kore this one   ⌊trols, restrains, represses

kore-ra these

kōri[1] ice

kōri[2] baggage

kōritsu public, municipal

korogarimas', korogaru rolls. tumbles

koroshimas'. korosu kills

koruku(-nuki) cork(-screw)

kōryo consideration, reflection

kōsa-ten an intersection (of streets)

kōsai social relations, company

koshi hips

koshi-kakemas', -kakeru sits down

koshimaki loincloth : petticoat

koshimas', kosu goes over ; exceeds

koshiraemas', koshiraeru makes, builds

koshō[1] 1. damage, something wrong 2. hin-
koshō[2] pepper ⌊drance, impediment

kōshō negotiations ; connections

kōshū the public, the masses

... koso indeed (it is ...)

kosu (koshimas') goes over ; exceeds

kōsui perfume

kosurimas', kosuru rub, scrape

kotaemas', kotaeru answers

Kōtaishi sama the Crown Prince

kotchi = kochira

koto thing, matter ; fact ; case ; experience
... (suru) koto ga aru does do it ; does
it sometimes ; ... (suru) koto ga nai
never does it ; ... (sh'ta) koto ga aru has
done it ; ... (sh'ta) koto ga nai has never
done it

kotoba 1. word, words ; sentence (spoken)
2. speech 3. language

kotonarimas', kotonaru is different, differs

koto-ni especially : moreover, what is more

kotoshi this year

kotowarimas', kotowaru 1. refuses, declines, begs off 2. makes excuses

kotowaza a proverb ⌈one)

kotozuke, kotozute a message (for some-
kōtsū communication ; traffic

kottō-hin curios, antiques

kowai 1. afraid ; frightful 2. terrific, swell

kowaremas', kowareru it breaks

kowashimas', kowasu breaks it

koya hut, shed

koyama hill

koyōji toothpick

kō yū this sort of, such

kōzan a mine

kozara saucer

kōzen open(ly), public(ly)

kozuchi a small hammer

kozukai¹ janitor ; attendant ; servant

kozukai² pin money, pocket money

kozutsumi package, parcel

ku¹ nine

ku² a ward (in a city)   ⌈deals (cards)

kubarimas', kubaru distributes, allots ;

kubetsu difference ; discrimination

kubi neck

kubomi hollow, dent, depression

kuchi 1. mouth 2. words, speech 3. entrance ; hole, opening 4. cork, stopper

kuchi-beni lipstick   ⌊5. job opening

kuchimas', kuchiru rots, decays

kuda pipe, tube

kudakemas', kudakeru it breaks, it smashes

kudakimas', kudaku breaks it, smashes it

kudamono fruit

175

kudari down, going down; descent

kudarimas', kudaru comes (goes) down;
... **kudasai** please ⌊falls, drops

kudasaimas', kudasaru gives; does the favor of

kudashi a purgative, a laxative; a vermifuge

kudoi 1. long-winded, dull 2. thick, greasy

kufū device, scheme

kugatsu September

kugi nail

kugiri punctuation

kūgun air force

kui post, stake, pile

kuimas', kuu eats

kuji a lot (in a lottery)

kujira whale

kuki stalk, stem

kūki air

kuma bear

kumi a set, suit, pack; a class, band, com-
kumiai association, guild, union ⌊pany

kumiawase assortment, mixture

kumimas' kumu ladles, scoops up; considers, sympathize

kumitate structure, set-up, organization,
kumo¹ cloud ⌊frame-work
kumo² spider

kumorimas', kumoru gets cloudy

... **kun** young Mr. ...

kuni 1. country 2. native place, home area

kura[1] saddle

kura[2] warehouse, storeroom, cellar

kurabemas', kuraberu compares, contrasts

kurabu club

kurai[1] dark, gloomy

kurai[2] 1. grade, rank 2. situation; fix; as much as; to the extent; about, approximately

kurashimas', kurasu lives, gets by, makes a living

kurasu class

kuremas', kureru[1] gives; does the favor of

kuremas', kureru[2] gets dark

kuri chestnut

kuriimu cream

kuriiningu cleaning

kurimas', kuru winds, reels

Kurisumasu Christmas

kurō difficulties, hardships

kuroi black

kurōto expert, professional

kuru[1] (**kimas'**) comes

kuru[2] (**kurimas'**) winds, reels

kuruimas', kuruu goes mad, insane; gets warped; gets out of order

kuruma car; taxi; vehicle

kurushii painful; hard, heavy

kusa, k'sa grass, weed

kusai, k'sai smelly, stinking; fishy, questionable

177

kusari, k'sari chain
kusarimas', kusaru goes bad, rots, decays
kuse, k'se a habit
kushami, k'shami a sneeze
kushi 1. a comb 2. a skewer, a spit
kuso, k'so dung, excrement
kusugurimas', kusuguru tickles
kusuguttai ticklish
kusuri, k'suri medicine
kusuri-ya, k'suri-ya drugstore
kutabiremas', kutabireru gets tired
kutsu shoes
kutsu-bera shoehorn
kutsu-himo shoelace
kutsu-migaki shoeshine
kutsu-naoshi shoe-repairman
kutsu-shita, kutsu-sh'ta socks
kuttsukimas', kuttsuku sticks to
kuu (kuimas') eats; bites
kuwa¹ hoe
kuwa² mulberry
kuwaemas', kuwaeru adds; imposes
kuwashii detailed
kuzu waste, trash, rags
kuzushimas', kuzusu 1. cashes, changes, breaks (into small money) 2. breaks down, demolishes 3. simplifies
kyabarē cabaret, nightclub
kyabetsu cabbage

kyaku (o-kyaku) visitor, guest, customer
kyandē candy
kyarameru caramels
kyatsu = koitsu
kyō today
kyōdai brothers and sisters ; brother ; sister
kyōdō union, cooperation, joint
kyōgi[1] game, match, contest
kyōgi[2] conference, discussion
kyōiku education
kyōju professor
kyōkai church
kyoku office, bureau
kyokuba circus
kyokutō Far East
kyōmi interest
kyonen last year
kyori distance
Kyōsan-shugi (-shugisha) Communism, (-ist)
kyōshi teacher, instructor, tutor
kyōshitsu classroom, schoolroom
kyōsō competition, rivalry, contest
kyōtsū common, general
kyōyō[1] for common use, for public use
kyōyō[2] culture, education, refinement
kyū class, grade
kyūji waiter, waitress, steward, office-boy
kyūkō express (train, etc)
kyūri cucumber

kyūyo compensation, allowance, grant

M

ma room ; space ; time ; leisure
mā well ; I should say ; perhaps
machi town
machigai mistake
machimas', matsu waits for
mada (not) yet ; still
madara spots, spotted, polka dots
...made until ; as far as ; to
mado window
mae front ; in front of ; before
magarimas', magaru 1. turns, goes around
   2. it bends, curves
magemas', mageru bends it, curves it
mago grandchild
mahi paralysis
mai- each
maiasa every morning
maiban every night
maido every time
maigo lost ; a lost child
mainen every year
mainichi every day ; all the time
mairimas', mairu 1. I come, I go 2. visits,
   calls on 3. is defeated, loses (a game, etc.)
maisō burial   ⌊4. is floored, stumped

Maitta! You've got me!

majime serious, sober

majirimas', majiru mixes

majiwarimas', majiwaru associates with

makasemas', makaseru entrust with, leaves in one's hands

makashimas', makasu 1. beats down the price 2. defeats

makemas', makeru 1. comes down on the price 2. loses, is defeated 3. is inferior

maki[1] firewood

maki[2] a roll; a volume

maki-e raised lacquer

makimas', maku rolls up; winds; wraps

makoto sincere; faithful; true; genuine

makura pillow

...mama as it is; as one wants

mame[1] beans

mame[2] blister, corn, bunion

mamorimas', mamoru defends, protects

man 10,000

man- fully

mane imitation

manekimas', maneku invites

manga cartoon, comics

man-ichi if by any chance

man-in full (of people)

mannaka the very middle

mannenhitsu fountain pen

Manshū Manchuria

181

manukaremas', manukareru escape from,
  be exempt from

manzai cross-talk comedy

mare rare

mari ball

maru circle, ring ; zero

maru- fully

maru de perfectly, completely

marui round

masarimas', masaru surpasses, is superior

machimas', matsu waits for

massaka-sama head over heels

massugu straight

masu (mashimas') increases, raises, swells

mata¹ again ; moreover

mata² groin ; crotch

mata-wa or, or else ; also

matchi match

mato aim, target   ⌈ranged, finished

matomarimas', matomaru is settled, ar-
matomemas', matomeru settles, arranges

matsu¹ pine tree

matsu² (machimas') waits for

matsuri a festival

mattaku quite, completely

mawarimas', mawaru goes around

mawashimas', mawasu turns around, passes around   ⌈gets perplexed

mayoimas', mayou gets lost ; gets dazed ;

182

mayu 1. eyebrows 2. cocoon

mazu first of all, before anything else

mazui 1. untasty 2. awkward, poor 3. in-

mazushii poor, needy ⌊advisable 4. ugly

me 1. eye 2. bud

-me -th (**itsutu-me** "5th") ⌈order

mechamecha in pieces, all confused, in dis-

medetai 1. auspicious, happy 2. simple-

megane eyeglasses ⌊minded

mei niece ⌈tion, a famous product

meibutsu a local speciality, a special attrac-

meijin expert

meirei order, command

meishi calling card

meishi-ire calling card case

meiwaku trouble, annoyance

meiyo prestige, honor, glory

mekata weight

mekura blind

men[1] mask ; surface ; front

men[2] cotton

mendō trouble, difficulty, nuisance

menkai interview, meeting

meriyasu knitted goods

meshi cooked rice ; a meal ⌈drinks

meshiagarimas', meshiagaru 1. eats 2.

meshimas', mesu in formal speech can re-
place such verbs as *kimas'* (wears), *tabemas'* (eats), *nomimas'* (drinks), etc.

meshitsukai servant

me-tsuki a look (in one's eyes)

metta reckless, rash

metta ni+NEGATIVE VERB seldom

mezamashi (-dokei) alarm clock

mezurashii rare, uncommon, novel, curious

mi 1. fruit, nut 2. body

mi(-) INFINITIVE OF *miru* (seeing)

mibun social standing

miburi gesture, movement

michi street, road

michimas', michiru is complete, is full

midare disorder

midashimas', midasu throws into disorder

midori green ⌐ 2. shows up, comes

miemas', mieru 1. is visible, can be seen

migakimas', migaku polishes, shines

migi right

migoto splendid, beautiful

migurushii unseemly, unsightly

mihon a sample

mijikai short (not long)

mikan tangerine ⌐point

mikata 1. a friend, an accomplice 2. a view-

mikka 3 days; 3rd day ⌐3. opinion

mikomi 1. promise, hope 2. expectation

mimai a visit (especially of sympathy, etc.)

mimas', miru sees, looks; tries doing

mimi ear

mimi-wa earring
mina-san you all, everybody
minami south
mine peak, summit
minkan the people ; civilians ; civil
mino straw raincoat
minori crop, harvest
minshu-shugi democracy
minshū the masses, the people
min-yō folk song, ballad
minzoku race
mirin sweet saké
miru (mimas') sees, looks ; tries doing
miruku milk
mise store, shop
misemas', miseru shows
misemono exhibition, exhibit
mishin sewing machine
miso bean paste
misu bamboo blind
mitashimas', mitasu fills up, satisfies
mitomemas', mitomeru recognizes, admits
mitsukarimas', mitsukaru is found, discovered
mitsukemas', mitsukeru finds, discovers
mittsu three
miukemas', miukeru observes, happens to
miya a Shinto shrine ⌊see
miyage a present, a souvenir

185

miyako capital, city

mizo drain, ditch

mizu (cold) water

mizuumi a lake

... mo also, too

... mo ... mo both...and...; neither... nor...

mō 1. already ; now 2. more

mochi rice cake

mochimas', motsu has, holds, carries

mochiron of course ⌐back, returns

modoshimas', modosu 1. vomits 2. sends

mohan model, pattern

moji letter, character, writing

mōkemas', mōkeru[1] makes money, profits

mōkemas', mōkeru[2] prepares, sets up

Mōko Mongolia

mokuhan woodblock print

mokuhyō target, goal

mokuroku catalog, list, table, inventory

mokutan charcoal

mokuteki aim, objective, purpose

mokuyōbi Thursday

mokuyoku bathing

momen cotton

momiji 1. maples 2. autumn leaves

monimas', momu massages; rubs; pounds on

momo 1. peach 2. hip, thigh

mon[1] family crest

mon[2] gate

mondai question, problem, topic

mon(o) 1. thing 2. person

...(sh'ta) mon(o) des' used to...

... mono because

mono- (emphatic prefix with adjectives)

monogatari a tale, a legend

monozuki curious, inquisitive

moppara principally, chiefly

moraimas', morau receives, gets ; has some one do for one

morashimas', morasu lets leak ; reveals

moremas', moreru leaks out ; is omitted

mori woods, forest

morimas', moru piles it up, accumulates it

moroi brittle, frail

mōru lace

moshi if

moshi moshi ! hello! hey! say!

mōshikomi application

mōshimas', mōsu 1. I say 2. I do

moto 1. origin, source 2. (at the) foot (of)

motomemas', motomeru 1. wants, looks for 2. asks for 3. buys, gets

moto-yori from the beginning ; by nature

motozukimas', motozuku is based on ; conforms to

motsu (mochimas') has, holds, carries

mottai-nai 1. is undeserving 2. it is waste-ful

motte ikimas' (iku) takes

motte imas' (iru) has, holds

motte kimas' (kuru) brings

motto more, still more; longer

motto-mo 1. most, exceedingly 2. indeed, of course 3. but, however

moyō pattern

mucha unreasonable; reckless; disorderly

muchi a whip

muchū trance, ecstasy

muda futile, no good, wasteful; useless

mudan de without notice, without permission

mugi grain; wheat, barley

mugiwara straw

mugoi cruel, brutal

muika 6 days; the 6th day

mujaki naive, innocent, unsophisticated

mujō heartless

mujun inconsistent; contradiction

mukaemas', mukaeru meets; welcomes; invites

mukaimas', mukau opposes; heads for

mukashi ancient times

mukimas', muku 1. faces 2. skins, pares

muko son-in-law; bridegroom

mukō opposite, across the way; over there (in America, etc.)

mukuimas', mukuiru repays; compensates

mumei nameless, anonymous

munashii empty; futile, in vain

mune[1] chest, breast; heart, mind

mune[2] purport, effect, intent

188

mura village

mure group, throng, flock

muri (shimas') (is) unreasonable, violent; overdoes; asking too much

muryō free of charge

mushi insect; worm

mushi-atsui muggy, close, sultry, humid

mushi-ba decayed tooth

mushi-kudashi vermifuge, worm remedy

mushimas', musu steams; is sultry, humid

musubimas', musubu ties; ties up, winds ⌊up; wears a tie

musuko, mus'ko son

musume daughter; girl

muttsu six

muyō unnecessary; useless; having no busi- ⌈ness

muzukashii hard, difficult

muzumuzu itchy, crawly, creepy

myō strange, queer

myōgonichi day after tomorrow

myōnichi tomorrow

N

n' = no

na[1] name

na[2] greens, vegetables

... **na !** isn't it, don't-you-know, you see

nabe pan, pot

nademas' naderu soothes, pets

189

nae seedling
nagai, nagaku long
...-nagara while ...-ing
nagaremas', nagareru flows
nagashi kitchen sink
nagashimas', nagasu lets flow
nagaya tenement house
nagekimas', nageku weeps, moans, laments
nagemas', nageru throws
nagurimas', naguru knock, beat, strike
nagusame comfort, consolation
nagusami amusement, entertainment
nai (arimasen) there is no..., has no ..., lacks
naichi inside the country, inland, internal
naifu knife ⌈approximately
naigai inside and out; home and abroad;
naikaku a government cabinet
naka 1. inside, in 2. relations, terms (be-
nakama friend, pal ⌊tween people)
nakanaka extremely (long, hard, bad, etc.),
  more than one might expect
...-nakereba unless
...-nakereba narimasen must, has to
nakimas', naku weeps; cries; makes an
naku(te) without ⌊animal sound
nama 1. raw, uncooked; fresh 2. hard cash
namae name
namaiki impertinent
namakemas', namakeru idles, is lazy

190

namari 1. lead (metal) 2. dialect, accent
Nambei South America
namboku north and south
nambu the south, the southern part
namemas', nameru licks, tastes
nami[1] ordinary, common, average
nami[2] wave
namida tear
nana(tsu) seven   ⌈agonal
naname slanting, oblique, at an angle, di-
nan(i) what
nan-, nam- how many...
nan dai = nan des' ka what is it
nan de mo anything at all
nanibun anyway, anyhow   ⌈don't want to
nan-nara if you prefer, if you like; if you
nan no what (kind of); of what
nanoka 7 days; the 7th day
nao still more; moreover   ⌈cured, fixed
naorimas', naoru is corrected, repaired,
naoshimas', naosu corrects, repairs, cures,
... nara if   ⌊fixes
narabemas', naraberu arranges, lines them
up   ⌈themselves
narabimas', narabu they line up, arrange
naraimas', narau learns
narashimas', narasu 1. smoothes, averages
2. domesticates, tames 3. sounds, rings it
naremas', nareru gets used to, grows

familiar with

nari form; personal appearance

narimas', naru[1] becomes, gets to be, turns into; is completed; is, amounts to

narimas', naru[2] (fruit) is borne

narimas', naru[3] it sounds, rings

naru-hodo I see; quite so; you are so right

nasake affection, feeling, tenderness, com-
nashi pear   ⌊passion

...-nashi without

nashimas', nasu achieves, forms, does

nasu eggplant

nata hatchet

natsu summer

natsu-mikan Japanese grapefruit

nawa rope, cord

naya barn, shed

nayami suffering, distress, torment

naze why

nazo riddle

ne 1. root 2. sound 3. sleeping 4. price

...ne! (nē!) isn't it, don't-you-know, you

nebari stickiness   ⌊see

negaimas', negau asks for, requests, begs

neji screw

neji-mawashi screwdriver

neko cat

nekutai necktie

nemas', neru goes to bed, lies down, sleeps

192

nemmatsu the end of the year

nemui sleepy

nemurimas', nemuru sleeps

nen¹ year

nen² deliberation, attention

nenryō fuel

neraimas', nerau aims at, watches for, seeks

neru¹ (nemas') goes to bed, lies down, sleeps

neru² (nerimas') kneads

neru flannel

nē-san big sister ; Miss ; Waitress !

netsu fever ; heat

neuchi value, worth

nezumi mouse, rat

ni¹ two

ni² load, burden

... ni in, at ; to ; for ; with ; and

niaimas', niau is becoming, suits

nibui dull

Nichi- Japanese

nichiyōbi Sunday

ni-do two times

niemas', nieru it boils, it cooks ⌈away

nigashimas', nigasu turns loose ; lets get

nigemas', nigeru runs away, escapes

nigirimas', nigiru grasps, grips, clutches

nigiyaka merry, bustling, lively, flourishing

Nihon Japan

Nihon-jin a Japanese

Nihongo Japanese (language)

Nihon-sei made in Japan

nii-san big brother

niji rainbow

ni-jū 1. twenty 2. double, duplicate

nikai 1. second floor, upstairs 2. two times

nikibi pimple

nikoniko smiling

niku meat

nikui dislikable, hated; hard, difficult

nikutai flesh, the body

nikuya butcher

nimas'[1], **niru** resembles

nimas'[2], **niru** boils, cooks

nimotsu baggage, load

nimpu coolie, workman

-nin person

ninaimas', **ninau** carries on shoulders

ningen human being

ningyō doll ⌐heartedness

ninjō human nature, human feelings, warm-

ninki popularity

ninsoku coolie, workman

ninshin pregnancy

ninshin-chūzetsu abortion

nioi a smell

nira a leek; a green onion

niramimas', **niramu** glares, stares

niru[1] (**nimas'**) boils, cooks

194

niru[2] (nimas') resembles

nise phony, imitation

nishiki brocade

nishin herring

nisu varnish

ni-tō 2nd class

niwa garden

niwatori chicken

no (no-hara) field

... no 1. SUBORDINATING PARTICLE: of, pertaining to, in, at 2. = **da** which is 3. the one 4. (= **koto**) the fact, the act

nobashimas', nobasu; nobemas', noberu[1] extends it, reaches; spreads it

nobemas', noberu[2] tells, relates ⌈spreads

nobimas', nobiru it extends, reaches; it

noborimas', noboru climbs, goes up

nodo throat

nodo ga kawakimash'ta is thirsty

nōgyō agriculture

no-hara field

nokemas', nokeru removes; omits

noki eaves

nokogiri a saw ⌈(over)

nokorimas', nokoru remains, is left behind

nokoshimas', nokosu leaves behind (over)

nokimas', noku gets out of the way

nomi[1] chisel

nomi[2] flea

nomimizu drinking water

nomimono beverage, something to drink

nōmin the farmers

nomimas', nomu drinks

nonki easygoing, happy-go-lucky

noren shop curtain ; credit

nori 1. paste ; starch 2. seaweed

norikaemas', norikaeru changes (trains, buses, etc.)

norimas', noru gets aboard, rides

nōritsu efficiency

noroi slow, dull   ⌈in

noru (norimas') gets aboard, rides ; is found

nosemas', noseru loads, puts aboard, ships ;

nōzei payment of taxes   ⌊publishes

. . . nozoite except for, with the exception of

nozokimas', nozoku 1. peeps at 2. removes, eliminates ; omits

nozomashii desirable, welcome

nozomimas', nozomu desires, looks to, hopes for ; looks out on   ⌈etc.)

nugimas', nugu takes off (clothes, shoes,

nuguimas', nuguu wipes away

nuimas', nuu sews   ⌈omitted

nukemas', nukeru comes off ; escapes ; is

nukimas', nuku uncorks ; removes ; omits ;

numa swamp, marsh   ⌊surpasses ; selects

nurashimas', nurasu wets, dampens

nuremas', nureru gets wet, damp

196

nuri lacquer, varnish, painting
nurimono lacquerware
nurimas', nuru lacquers, paints, varnishes
nurui lukewarm ; sluggish
nushi master, owner
nusumimas', nusumu steals, swipes, robs
nuu (nuimas') sews
nyūbai the rainy season
nyūgaku admission to a school, entering a ⌈school
nyūin entering a hospital, hospital admission
nyūjō-ken admission ticket
nyūsu news
nyūyō necessary, needed
nyūyoku bath, taking a bath

O

o¹ (=shippo) tail
o² thong, strap (=hanao)
... O DIRECT OBJECT PARTICLE
o- HONORIFIC PREFIX: "your" or "that common thing we often talk about"
ō- big, great
oba(san) aunt ; lady
obā(san) grandmother ; old lady
obi belt, sash
oboemas', oboeru remembers
obuimas', obuu carries on one's back
o-cha Japanese green tea

ochimas', ochiru falls; drops; is omitted; fails; runs away; is inferior ⌈cool

ochitsukimas', ochitsuku calms down, keeps

ōdan[1] jaundice

ōdan[2] crossing, going across, intersecting

odorimas', odoru dances

odorokimas', odoroku is surprised, aston-

oemas', oeru finishes, completes ⌊ished

ōfuku round trip ⌈respect

ogamimas', ogamu worships; looks at with

ōgata large-size (model)

ōgesa exaggerated

ogi a reed

ōgi a folding fan

oginaimas', oginau completes; complements; makes good, makes up for

ōgoe de in a loud voice ⌈person to

ogorimas', ogoru is extravagant; treats a

o-hachi a rice bucket

ohako hobby; specialty, trick

Ohayō (gozaimas')! Good morning!

o-hiya cold water

oi nephew

oi! hey!

oi, ōku many, numerous ⌈stays

oide (ni narimas') 1. comes 2. goes 3. is,

oimas', ou[1] chases, pursues

oimas', ou[2] carries on back

ōimas', ōu covers, shields

oiru (lubricating) oil (*for car*)

oishii tasty, nice, delicious

oji (san) uncle

o-jigi a polite bow

ojii-san grandfather

ojoku disgrace, shame, scandal

ojō-san a young lady; your daughter

oka hill; dry land

okabu = ohako

okage sama de thanks to your kind attitude; thank you (I'm very well *or* it's going very nicely).

okame moonfaced woman

okami landlady, woman

ōkami wolf

o-kane money

okāsan mother

okashii amusing, funny

okashimas', okasu commits, perpetrates; violates, encroaches upon

ōkata 1. for the most part 2. probably

o-kawari 1. a second helping 2. change (in health)

okazu side dishes (*anything but rice*)

oke tub, wooden bucket

oki offshore

...-oki ni at intervals of ...

okiba a place (to put something)

ōkii, ōki na big, large

okimas',[1] **oku** puts ; does for later
okimas',[2] **okiru** gets up
okimono an ornament ; bric-a-brac
o-kome rice
okonaimas', **okonau** acts, does, carries out, performs 「from
okorimas', **okoru**[1] 1. happens 2. springs
okorimas', **okoru**[2] gets mad (angry)
okoshimas', **okosu** raises ; establishes ; gets a person up
okotarimas', **okotaru** neglects; is lazy about
ok'-san wife
oku[1] a hundred million
oku[2] the back or inside part
oku[3] (**okimas'**) puts ; does for later
ōku lots ; mostly
okubi belch 「runs slow
okuremas', **okureru** is late ; falls behind ;
okurimono gift, present
okurimas', **okuru** 1. presents, awards with 2. sends ; sees a person off ; spends (time)
omake extra, bonus, premium; to boot
omaru bed-pan ; chamberpot
omawari-san policeman 「on back
ombu (**shimas'**) carries baby on back ; rides
omedetō (**gozaimas'**) congratulations; happy new year 「3. invites
omeshi (**ni narimas'**) 1. wears 2. buys
omocha toy

omoi heavy ; important

omoi-dashimas', -dasu remembers, recollects

omoimas', omou thinks, feels

omo na principal, main

omoshiroi interesting, pleasant, amusing, fun

omou thinks, feels

ōmu a parrot

omuretsu omelet

omutsu diapers

on[1] obligation ; kindness

on[2] sound ; pronunciation

onaji same

onaka stomach

onaka ga s'kimash'ta is hungry

onara flatulence, wind

ondo temperature

ongaku music

oni devil, ogre

onna woman, female

ono ax, hatchet

onore self

onozukara automatically, spontaneously

onsen hot spring

ōrai[1] traffic ; communication ; thoroughfare

ōrai[2] "all right" (all clear, go ahead)

Oranda Holland, Dutch

orenji orange, orange drink

oremas' oreru it breaks ; it folds

ori[1] time, occasion

ori[2] cage ; jail

orime fold, crease, pleat

orimono textiles, cloth

orimas', oriru gets down, gets off

orimas', oru[1] is, stays=(**imas', iru**)

orimas', oru[2] breaks (folds, bends) it

orimas', oru[3] weaves

oroshimas', orosu takes down ; unloads ; invests ; drops (from a car), lets out (of vehicle) ⌈trols

osaemas', osaeru represses, restrains, con-

o-sake=**sake**[1]

osamemas', osameru 1. reaps, harvests ; gets 2. pays ; finishes 3. governs ; pacifies

oseji compliment, flattery

oshaberi chatterbox, gossip

oshare dandy, fancy dresser

oshiemas', oshieru teaches, shows, tells,

oshii 1. regrettable 2. precious ⌊informs

oshiire closet, cupboard

oshimas', osu pushes

oshiroi face powder

Ōshū, Europe

osoi late ; slow

osoreirimas' 1. excuse me 2. thank you

osoremas', osoreru fears

osoroshii fearful, dreadful

osshaimas', ossharu (someone honored) says ; is called

osu (oshimas') pushes
Ōs'torariya Australia
oto sound, noise
otoko man, male, boy
otona adult
otonashii gentle, well-behaved
otori decoy ; lure ⌈weak
otoroemas', otoroeru declines, fades, grows
otorimas', otoru is inferior, worse
otoshimas', otosu drops
otōto younger brother
ototoi day before yesterday
ototoshi year before last
otsu chic, stylish
ou (oimas')[1] chases, pursues
ou (oimas')[2] carries on back
ōu (ōimas') covers, shields
owarimas', owaru it ends
oya parent
oya-bun boss, ringleader, chief
ōyake public, open, official
oyatsu snack (esp. mid-afternoon)
ōyō application, putting to use
oyobi and also
oyobimas', oyobu reaches, extends to, equals
oyogimas', oyogu swims
ō-yorokobi de with great delight
oyoso about, roughly
ōzei large crowd, throng

P

pa ...! all gone ; boom !
pachinko pinball
pāma permanent wave
pan bread
panku puncture, blowout
pan-s'ke pompom girl
pan-ya bakeshop
paripari crisp ; first-rate
pēji page
penki paint
pikapika flashing, glittering
pinto focus
poketto pocket
pomādo pomade, hair oil
pombiki a pimp, a hustler
posuto, pos'to a mailbox
potsu a dot
puro-resu professional wrestling ⌐ing lot
pūru 1. swimming pool 2. motor pool, park-

R

-ra and others ; all of
raigetsu next month
raikyaku guest, caller, visitor
rainen next year

raishū next week

rajio radio

raku ease, comfort, comfortable

rakudai failure (in a test)

rakugaki scribbling ; doodling

rambō violence, outrage ; disorderly

rāmen Chinese noodles

ramma transom window (opening)

ramune lemonade

ran 1. orchid 2. column

ranchi 1. lunch 2. launch

randoseru knapsack

rappa trumpet

... rashii probably ; it seems like ; it looks like

rebā 1. liver 2. lever

rei[1] (o-rei) greeting ; thanks

rei[2] (maru) zero

rei[3] precedent, example

reibō (-sōchi) air conditioning

reigai exception (to the rule)

reigi courtesy

reizōko refrigerator, icebox

rekishi history

rekōdo record

remon lemon

ren-ai love

renchū gang, crowd, clique

renga brick

rengō union, alliance, Allied

renraku connection; relevancy
renshū training, practice, drill
ressha a train
retsu row, line
rettō archipelago, chain of islands
ri advantage, profit, interest
rieki benefit, advantage, profit
rihatsu-ten barbershop
rikai understanding, comprehension
rikō clever, sharp
riku land
rikugun army
rikutsu reason, logic, argument
rin a bell, a doorbell
ringo apple
rinji extraordinary, special, emergency
rinki emergency; expedient
rippa fine, splendid; well
rireki personal history, summary of one's ⌈career
rishi interest
risō ideal
risu squirrel
ritsu 1. rate, proportion 2. a cut, a per-
rittai solid; 3-D, stereoscopic ⌊centage
riyō use, utilization
riyū reason
rōdō-sha worker, laborer
roji alley
rōka passage, corridor, aisle

roku six

Rōma Rome

rōma-ji romanization, Latin letters

ron argument, discussion; treatise

rōnin an unemployed samurai; a boy between schools; a man without a job

ronri logic

Roshiya Russia

rōsoku candle

rōsu-biifu roastbeef

rōzu waste, refuse; damaged goods

rumpen tramp, hobo

rusu 1. absent, away from home 2. taking care of the house while one is away

rusu-ban someone to take care of the house in one's absence   ⌈ens; omits

ryakushimas', ryakusu abbreviates, short-

ryō 1. hunting; fishing (as sport) 2. dormitory, boardinghouse 3. mound, mausoleum 4. territory 5. quantity.

ryōgae money exchange

ryōhō both

ryōji (-kan) consul(ate)

ryokan inn

ryoken passport

ryokō travel, trip

ryokyaku traveler, passenger

ryōri cooking

ryōri-ten, -ya a restaurant

ryōshin[1] both parents
ryōshin[2] conscience
ryūkō popularity, vogue
Ryūkyū the Ryukyus (Okinawa, etc.)

S

sā well ; come on
...sa! EMPHATIC PARTICLE
sabi rust
sabishii lonely
sābisu service ; free (as part of the service)
saborimas', saboru cuts class; plays hookey
sadamarimas', sadamaru is settled, fixed
sadamemas', sadameru settles it, fixes it
...sae even ; only ⌐down
sagarimas', sagaru it hangs down ; goes
sagashimas', sagasu it looks for
sagemas', sageru 1. lets it hang down ;
  lowers 2. carries (hanging)
sagurimas', saguru gropes
sai[1] talent, ability
sai[2] side-dish
sai[3] time, occasion
sai[4] wife
saiban trial, court decision
saichū midst
saifu purse
saigo last, final

saijō best, highest
saiku work(manship), ware
saishin newest, up-to-date
saisho the very beginning (first)
saishū final, the very end (last)
saiwai good fortune
saji spoon
saka hill, slope
sakan flourishing, prosperous; vigorous splendid,
sakana 1. fish 2. appetizers with liquor
sakasama upside down
sakazuki wine cup, saké cup
sake[1] saké (Japanese rice-wine)
sake[2] salmon
sakebimas', sakebu cries out, shouts
sakemas', sakeru avoids
saki 1. front; future; ahead 2. point, tip
saki-hodo a little while ago
sakimas', saku blooms, blossoms
sakku condom
sakura cherry tree
sakurambo a cherry
sam- =**san-**
...sama =**...san** Mr., Mrs., Miss ...ers
samatagemas', samatageru obstructs, hind-
samayoimas', samayou wanders about
sama-zama diverse, all kinds
samemas', sameru[1] wakes up, comes to one's senses

209

samemas', sameru² gets cold, cools off

sampo a walk

samui cold, chilly

san three

-san 1. Mr., Mrs., Miss 2. mountain

sangyō industry

sanka participation

sankaku triangle

sansei approval, support

santō third class

sao pole, rod

sappari 1. not at all 2. clean; fresh 3. frank

sara plate, dish; saucer; ashtray

sarada salad

saru monkey

sasemas', saseru makes (do), lets (do), has [(do)

sashi-agemas', -ageru presents; holds up

sashimas', sasu 1. points to; holds umbrella 2. stabs, stings

sasoimas', sasou invites; tempts

satō sugar

satsu¹ a volume, a book

satsu² paper money, a bill

satsujin murder

sawagimas', sawagu makes lots of noise, [clamors

sawarimas', sawaru touches

sayonara goodby

sebiro business suit

sei¹ height, stature

sei[2] 1. nature 2. sex

sei[3] cause ; due to...

-sei made in ...

seibu the west, the western part

seifu government

seifuku uniform

seiji politics

seikatsu life

seikō success

seinen young man, youth

seiryoku power, energy ; influence

seisan production, manufacture

seiseki results, marks

seishiki formal, formality

seishin soul, mind, spirit

seishitsu character, disposition

seito pupil, student

seitō political party ⌜America

seiyō the West, the Occident, Europe and

seizei at most, at best

seizō production, manufacture

seizon existence

sekai world

seken the public, people, the world

seki[1] cough

seki[2] seat

Sekijūji Red Cross

sekinin responsibility, obligation

sekitan coal

211

sekiyu kerosene, petroleum

sekkaku especially ; with much trouble

sekken soap

semai narrow

sembei rice-crackers

semete at least ; at most

semmenki wash basin

semmon specialty, major (line)

sempō the other side

sempūki electric fan

sen[1] thousand

sen[2] line, route

sen[3] plug, cork, stopper

sen[4] (**-to**) cents

senden propaganda, publicity

sengetsu last month

sengo postwar

sen-in member of the crew ; ship's crew

senji wartime

senkyo election

senryō military occupation

sensei teacher ; Dr. ....

senshu athlete ; champion

senshū last week

sensō war, battle

sentaku[1] washing, laundry

sentaku[2] selection, choice

senzen prewar

seppuku harakiri

seri auction

serifu one's lines (in a play), dialogue

sētā sweater

setomono pottery, chinaware

Seto-naikai The Inland Sea

setsubi equipment, facilities

setsumei explanation

setsuna moment, instant

sewa 1. care, trouble, assistance 2. meddling, minding other people's business

sewashii busy

-sha company

shaberimas', shaberu chatters

shabon soap

shaburimas', shaburu sucks, chews

shachō president of a company, boss

shadan corporation

shadō road, roadway, driveway

shagamimas', shagamu squats, crouches

sha-in employee   [on heels

shakai society, social

shakkuri hiccup

shako garage, car-barn

shan pretty, handsome

share joke, pun

shashin photo, picture

shashō conductor

shatsu undershirt

shawā shower

shi[1] death

shi[2] = yon four

shi[3] city

shi[4] poetry

... shi Mr. ...

... shi, and

shiagemas', shiageru finishes up

shiai match, contest, meet

shiasatte three days from now

shiawase luck, fortune

shiba 1. turf, lawn 2. brushwood

shibai play (drama)

shibaraku for a while   [again.

Shibaraku des' ne. It's nice to see you

shibarimas', shibaru ties up

shibashiba often, repeatedly

shibiremas', shibireru goes numb, (a leg,
     etc.) falls asleep

shibori, o-shibori a wet towel (wrung out)

shiborimas', shiboru wrings out, squeezes

shibui 1. puckery, astringent 2. wry; glum
     3. severely simple, tastefully bare

shichi[1] seven

shichi[2] something pawned

shichi-jū seventy

shichimen-chō turkey

shichiya pawnbroker, pawnshop

shichō mayor

shichū stew

shidai circumstances; as soon as
shidan army division
shidashiya caterer
shigai outskirts of city, suburbs
shigaretto cigarette
shigatsu April
shigeki stimulation
shigoto job, work, undertaking
shigure drizzle
shihai management, control
shiharai paying out
shihon capital, funds
shiji support, maintenance
shijin poet
shi-jū forty
shijū all the time
shika deer
...shika except for, only, but
shikaku, sh'kaku 1. square 2. qualification, competency
shikarimas', shikaru scolds
shikashi, sh'kashi but, however
shikata (sh'kata) ga arimasen there's nothing we can do about it
shiken, sh'ken examination, test
shikimono spread; a rug, a cushion
shikkari firmly, resolutely
shikki dampness
shikko urinate (child's word)

215

shikimas', shiku spreads; sits on
shima[1] island
shima[2] stripes
shimaimas', shimau puts away, finishes
shimas', suru does
shimasen doesn't
shimash'ta did
Shimatta! Damn!
shimbun newspaper
shimemas', shimeru closes
shimerimas', shimeru is damp
shimeshimas', shimesu shows, indicates
shimi stain, blot
shimimas', shimiru penetrates, smarts
shimin citizen
shimo frost
shimpai worry, uneasiness
shimpo progress
shin 1. core, pith, heart 2. heart, spirit
shina articles, goods; quality
Shina China
shindai bed, berth
shingō signal
shinimas', shinu dies
shinja a believer; a Christian
shinjimas', shinjiru believes in, trusts
shinju pearl
shinkei nerve
shinnen new year

shinobimas', shinobu bears, puts up with
shinrai trust, confidence
shinri 1. psychology 2. truth
shinrui relative
shinsatsu medical examination
shinsetsu kind, cordial
shinu (shinimas') dies
shin-yō trust, confidence; credit
shinzō heart
shio 1. salt 2. tide
shippai failure, blunder. defeat
shippo tail
shirabemas', shiraberu investigates, ex-
⌐amines
shirami louse
shirase report, notice
shireikan commandant, headquarters
shiri buttocks, bottom, seat
shirimas', shiru knows
shiro (o-shiro) castle
shiroi white
shirōto amateur
shiru¹ juice, gravy; broth, soup
shiru² (shirimas') knows
shirushi indication, sign, symptom; effect
shiryo consideration, thought(-fulness)
shishi lion
shisō thought, concept
shita, sh'ta¹ bottom, below, under
shita, sh'ta² tongue

217

shita, sh'ta[3] did, has done
shitagatte according to, in conformity with
shitaku, sh'taku preparation, arrangement
shitashii intimate, familiar
shitate-ya tailor
shite, sh'te doing; does and
shiten branch shop
shitsu quality, nature
shitsubō disappointment
shitsugyō unemployment
shitsumon question
shitsurei discourtesy, impoliteness
shitsuren disappointment in love
shitte imas' knows
shiwa wrinkle, crease, fold
shiwaza act, deed ⌐way
shiyō 1. use, employment 2. method, means,
shizen nature, natural
shizuka quiet, still
shizumimas', shizumu sinks
shō nature, disposition, quality
shōbai trade, business
shōben urine, urinate
shōbō fire-fighting
shōbu match, game, contest ⌐dealing with
shobun, shochi management, disposition,
shōchi agreement
Shōchi shimash'ta. Yes, sir.
shōchō symbol

shōga ginger
shōgai impediment, obstacle, hindrance
shōgakkō primary (elementary) school
shōgakusei primary school children
shōgi chess
shōgyō commerce, trade
shōhi consumption, spending
shōhin goods, merchandise
shoimas', shou carries on back, shoulders
shōjiki honest
shoki secretary
shōki sober; in one's right mind
shōkin 1. hard cash 2. prize money; reward
  3. indemnity, reparation
shokki table service (ware)
shokki-dana pantry, dish-cupboard
shokkō factory-worker; workman
shōko proof, evidence
shōkō commissioned officer
shoku 1. office, occupation 2. food
shokubutsu (botanical) plant
shokudō dining room; restaurant
shokudō-sha dining car, diner
shokuen table salt
shokugyō occupation, profession
shokuhin groceries
shokuji meal
shokumotsu food
shokuryō-hin groceries

shokuyoku appetite
shomei signature
shōnen boy, lad, youngster
shōni infant, child
shōnin merchant, trader
shōrai future ⌐tion
shōrei encouragement, stimulation, promo-
shori managing, disposing of, transacting,
shōryaku abbreviation ⌊dealing with
shōsa major; lieutenant commander
shosai study, library (room)
shoseki books, publications
shōsetsu fiction, novel
shōshō = chotto
shōsoku news, word from
shotai housekeeping; a household
shōtai invitation
shotchū all the time
shoten bookshop
shōten focus
shotō islands
shotoku income, gain
shotoku-zei income tax
shōtotsu collision
shou (shoimas') carries on back, shoulders
shōyo bonus, prize, reward
shoyū possession, one's own
shōyu soy sauce
shozai whereabouts

220

shū(-kan) week

shuchō shimas' asserts, claims, maintains

shudan ways, means, measures, steps

shūdan group, collective body

shufu 1. housewife 2. capital city

shugeki attack, charge

shugi principle, doctrine, -ism

shūi circumference; surroundings

shujin boss, master; husband

shuju all kinds of

shujutsu operation, surgery

shūkan custom, practice, habit

shukudai homework

shukuga congratulation

shū-kuriimu a cream puff, an eclair

shūmai small Chinese meat-filled pastries

shūmatsu weekend

shumi taste, interest

shunkan a moment, an instant

shuppan publishing

shuppatsu departure

shūri repair

shurui kind, sort

shūsen(-go) (after) the end of the war

shūshin ethics, morals

shūshoku getting a job

shusse making a success out of life

shusseki attendance, presence

shutchō a business trip, an official tour

shūten terminus
shuyō leading, chief
shūzen repair
sō 1. that's right, yes 2. that way, like that
Sō des' ka. 1. Oh? How interesting! 2. Is that right?
soba[1] side, near
soba[2] (**o-soba**) buckwheat noodles
sōbetsu farewell; send-off
soboku simple, naive, unsophisticated
sōchi equipment, apparatus
sochira 1. there, that way 2. that one
sōdan consultation, conference, advice, talk
sodatemas', sodateru raises, rears, educates
sodachimas', sodatsu grows up, is raised (reared)
sode sleeve
soemas', soeru adds, throws in extra, attaches
sofu grandfather
sofuto(-kuriimu) "soft ice cream" = frozen custard
sōgo mutual, reciprocal
sōi discrepancy, difference
soimas', sou runs along, follows
soitsu that one
sōji cleaning, sweeping
sōji-fu cleaning lady (man)
sōji-ki a sweeper
sōjū shimas' manipulates, handles, controls, operates
sōkei the grand total
sokki shorthand

sokkuri entirely, completely; just like

soko[1] there, that place

soko[2] bottom

sokudo, sokuryoku speed

sokutatsu special delivery

somatsu crude, coarse

somemas', someru dyes

son damage, loss, disadvantage

sonaemas', sonaeru prepares, fixes, installs, furnishes; possesses

songai damage, harm

sonkei respect, esteem

sonna such (a), that kind of

sonnara then, in that case

sono that

son-shimas', -suru 1. incurs loss 2. exists

sonzai existence

soppa buckteeth

sora sky

sora de by heart, from memory [2. warps

sorashimas', sorasu 1. dodges, turns aside

sore that one, it

soremas', soreru deviates, strays, digresses

Soren Soviet Russia

sori 1. warp, curve, bend 2. sled

sōri-daijin prime minister, premier

sorimas', soru 1. shaves 2. bends, warps

sōritsu establishment

soroban abacus, counting beads

soroemas', soroeru puts in order; collects;
soroi a set of something ⌊completes a set
soroimas', sorou are arranged in order;
  gather together; make a set
sōron quarrel, dispute
sorosoro little by little
soru (sorimas') 1. shaves 2. bends, warps
soshiki system, structure
sōshiki funeral
soshō lawsuit
sōshoku ornament, decoration
sosogimas', sosogu pours (into)
sōsu sauce; gravy
sotchi = sochira
soto outside, outdoors
sōtō 1. rather, quite, fairly 2. suitable, prop-
  ...(ni) **sotte** along the ...   ⌐er
sou (soimas') runs along, follows
sōzō imagination
su 1. nest 2. vinegar
sū number; numeral
suashi barefoot
subarashii wonderful
subekkoi slippery, slick, smooth
suberimas' suberu, slides, slips, skates
subete all
sue 1. end, close 2. future
sufu staple fiber
sūgaku mathematics

sugata form, figure, shape
sugi cryptomeria, Japanese cedar
. . .-sugi past (the hour)
sugimas', sugiru passes; exceeds; overdoes
sugoi 1. swell, wonderful, terrific 2. dread-
sugoku terribly ⌊ful, ghastly, weird
sugu ni at once, immediately ⌈ses
suguremas', sugureru is excellent; surpas-
suidō waterworks, water service
suiei swimming
suifu seaman, sailor
suigara cigarette (cigar) butt
suihei[1] navy man, sailor, seaman
suihei[2] horizon; water level ⌈in
suimas', suu sips, sucks, smokes, breathes
suimin(-zai) sleep(ing) pills)
suiyōbi Wednesday
suji tendon; muscle; fiber; line; plot
sūji numeral, figure
sukebe, s'kebe oversexed, wolfish
suki, s'ki[1] is liked
suki, s'ki[2]**(-ma)** crack; opening; opportunity
suki, s'ki[3] a plow
sukimas', suku 1. likes 2. plows 3. combs
sukkari completely, all
sukoshi, s'koshi a little, a bit
sukunai few, meager
sukuimas', sukuu helps, rescues, saves
sumai residence

225

sumashimas', sumasu 1. finishes, concludes 2. puts up with (things as they are)

sumi[1] an inside corner

sumi[2] 1. charcoal 2. India ink

sumō Japanese wrestling

sumimas', sumu 1. comes to an end 2. lives

Sumimasen. 1. Excuse me. 2. Thank you.

sumpō measurements

suna sand ⌈in other words

sunawachi namely, to wit; that is to say;

sune shin, leg

supōtsu, s'pōts' sports, athletics

suppai sour

suremas', sureru it rubs, grazes

suri pickpocket

surimas', suru 1. rubs; files; grinds 2. prints 3. picks one's pockets

suru (shimas') does

sushi (o-sushi) pickled-rice tidb

suso skirt (of mountain); hem

susu soot

susumemas', susumeru encourages, recommends, advises, persuades, urges

susumimas', susumu goes forward, progresses; goes too fast, gets ahead

sutando, s'tando a stand; gas station; desk lamp, floor lamp

suteki, s'teki fine, splendid, swell

sutekki, s'tekki walking stick, cane

226

sutemas', suteru throws away, abandons

sutēshon, s'tēshon railroad station

suto, s'to (sutoraiki) strike

sutōbu, s'tōbu stove, heater

suu (suimas') sips, sucks, smokes, breathes ⌈in

suwarimas', suwaru sits (especially Japa-

suzu 1. tin 2. little bells ⌊nese style)

suzume sparrow

suzushii cool

T

ta rice-field

taba bundle, bunch

tabako cigarettes; tobacco

tabemas', taberu eats

tabemono food

tabi[1] Japanese split-toe socks

tabi[2] journey, trip

... tabi ni every time...

tabi-tabi often

tabun 1. probably, likely; perhaps 2. a lot

tachi nature, disposition

tachiba viewpoint, standpoint, situation

tachi-domarimas', -domaru stops. stands

Tachiiri Kinshi No Trespassing ⌊still

tachimas'. tatsu 1 stands up; leaves 2.

⌊elapses 3. cuts off

tada 1. only, just 2. (for) free 3. ordinary

tadaima just now ; in a minute

Tadaima (kaerimashita)! I'm back! (said on returning to one's residence)

tadashii proper, correct, honest ⌐terruption

taema-naku, taezu continuously, without in-

taemas', taeru 1. bears, puts up with ; 2. ⌐ceases

taga a barrel hoop

tagai (ni) mutual(ly)

-tagarimas', -tagaru wants to, is eager to

tai- 1. versus, towards, against 2. big, great

tai[1] sea bream, red snapper

tai[2] form, style ; body

tai[3] belt ; zone

-tai wants to, is eager to

taifū typhoon

taigai 1. in general ; for the most part ; practically 2. probably, like, like as not

Taiheiyō Pacific Ocean

taihen 1. very, exceedingly, terribly 2. serious ; disastrous ; enormous

taii army captain ; navy lieutenant

taiiku physical education, athletics

taikai 1. ocean, high sea 2. mass meeting ; ⌐convention

taikaku body build, physique

taikei a system

taiken personal experience

taiko drum

taikutsu boring, dull

taiman negligent, careless, neglectful

taimen 1. sense of honor, "face" 2. inter- [view

taira even, smooth, flat

tairiku continent

taisa 1. army colonel; navy captain 2. a [great difference

Taiseiyō Atlantic Ocean

taisen a great war, a world war

taisetsu important; precious

taishi ambassador

taishi-kan embassy

tai-shita (-sh'ta) important; serious; im- [mense

... **ni tai-sh'te** against; toward

taishō 1. general; admiral 2. contrast

taishū the general public, the masses; pop- [ular

taisō calisthenics, physical exercises

Taiwan Formosa

taiya a tire

taiyō 1. ocean 2. sun 3. summary

taka 1. hawk 2. quantity

takai high; loud

takara a treasure

take bamboo

take-no-ko bamboo shoot

taki waterfall

taki-bi bonfire

taki-gi firewood, fuel

taki-tsuke kindling

takimas', taku makes a fire; cooks; burns

tako 1. octopus 2. kite 3. callus, corn

taku (takimas') makes a fire; cooks; burns

taku 1. house; husband 2. table, desk
takumi skill
tak'san, takusan lots
takuwaemas', takuwaeru saves up, hoards
tama 1. ball; globe; bulb; bullet 2. jewel;
  bead; drop 3. round thing; coin; slug
tama ni rarely, occasionally, seldom
tamago egg
tamaranai, tamarimasen can't stand it; is ⌐intolerable
tamarimas', tamaru it accumulates
tamashii soul, spirit
tamatama occasionally
tamatsuki billiards
tambo rice-field
tame 1. for the sake (good, benefit) of 2.
  for the purpose of 3. because (of)
tamemas', tameru accumulates it
tameshimas', tamesu tries, attempts, experi-
tammono draperies, dry goods ⌐ments with
tamoto sleeve; edge, end
tamochimas', tamotsu keeps, preserves
tampopo dandelion
tamushi ringworm; athlete's foot
tana shelf, rack
tane 1. seed 2. source, cause 3. material 4.
  secret, trick to it 5. subject, topic
tango words, vocabulary
tan-i unit
tani(-ma) valley

tanjōbi birthday

tanomimas', tanomu 1. begs, requests 2. relies upon; entrusts with 3. hires, engages (a professional man)

tanoshii pleasant, enjoyable

tanoshimimas', tanoshimu enjoys

tansan(-sui) soda water

tansu chest of drawers

tantei detective

tanuki 1. badger 2. sly person

tanzen = dotera padded bathrobe

taoremas', taoreru falls down, tumbles, **taoru** towel ⌊collapses

taoshimas', taosu knocks down, overthrows

tappuri fully, more than enough

tara cod (fish)

. . .-tara if

tarai tub, basin

tarappu gangway

tarashimas', tarasu 1. seduces; wheedles 2. hangs, dangles; drops, spills

taremas', tareru hangs down, dangles; drips

tarimas, tariru is enough, suffices

taru barrel, keg ⌈laxed

tarumimas', tarumu gets slack (loose), re-**taryō** large quantity

tashika, tash'ka for sure; safe

tashikamemas', tashikameru makes sure, **tassha** healthy; skillful, good at ⌊ascertains

231

tasshimas', tassuru accomplishes; reaches;

tasū large number; majority ⌐lieved

tasukarimas', tasukaru is saved; is re-

tasukemas', tasukeru 1. helps 2. saves

tasuki a sleeve cord

takaimas', tatakau fights

tatakimas'. tataku strikes, hits

tatami floor-matting

tatamimas', tatamu folds up

tate ni lengthwise, vertically

-tate (no) fresh from...

tate-fuda signboard

tate-mashi house extension, annex

tatemas'. tateru erects, builds; sets up.

tatemono building ⌊establishes

tatoeba for example, for instance ⌐off

tatsu 1. stands up; leaves 2. elapses 3. cuts

taue rice-planting

tawara straw bag; bale

tawashi scrubbing-brush; swab

tayori communication, correspondence, a
letter, word from

tayorimas', tayoru relies on, depends on

tazunemas', tazuneru 1. asks (a question)
2. visits 3. looks for

te hand, arm; trick, move; kind ⌐ing

...-te GERUND: does and, is and; doing, be-

teate treatment; reparation, provision; al-

tebukuro gloves ⌊lowance

tēburu table ; **-kake** table-cloth

tegakari a hold, a place to hold on ; a clue, the track of

tegami letter

tegata a note, a bill

te-gatai safe ; reliable ; steady

tegokoro discretion

teguchi way (of doing things), trick

tehazu arrangements

tehon model, pattern

tei- fixed, appointed

teian proposal, suggestion

teibō dike, embankment

teiden failure (stoppage) of electricity

teido degree, extent

teika the set price

teiki (no) fixed, regular, periodical

teikoku empire, imperial

teinei polite ; careful

te-ire repair ; upkeep

teisai appearance, get-up, form

teisha stopping (of a vehicle)

teishi suspension, interruption

teishoku the regular meal ; table d'hote

teishu host ; landlord ; husband

tejun order, procedure, program

tekazu trouble

teki enemy, opponent, rival

-teki a drop

tekido moderation

233

tekigi suitable, fit

tekisetsu appropriate, to the point

tekishimas'. tekisuru is suitable, qualified

tekis'to. tekisuto text (book)

tekitō suitable

tekki(-ten) hardware (store)

tekkyō iron bridge

teko lever

te-kubi wrist

tema time ; trouble

temae this side ; me, I

temane gesture

temaneki beckoning

temawari personal effects ; luggage

...-te mo even if...

tempi oven

tempura anything fried in batter, especially ⌈shrimp

ten 1. point, dot 2. sky, heaven

-ten shop ⌈person

tengu 1. a long-nosed goblin 2. conceited

te-nimotsu hand luggage

ten-in shop clerk

tenjō ceiling

tenki 1. weather 2. nice weather

tennen natural

Tennō (sama) the Emperor

tensai genius

tensei disposition, temperament

tenshi angel

te-nugui hand towel
te-ono hatchet
teppen top
teppō rifle
tēpu tape
tera Buddhist temple
terebi television
teremas', tereru feels embarrassed, awk- [ward, flustered
terimas', teru it shines
tesage handbag
tesū trouble
tetsu iron, steel
tetsudaimas', tetsudau helps
tetsudō railroad
tetsugaku philosophy
tetsuzuki formalities, procedure
tettei-teki thorough
to door
tō 1. ten 2. rattan, cane 3. tower, pagoda
tō- 1. the current, the appropriate 2. east
Tō-a East Asia
tobashimas', tobasu lets fly; skips, omits; [hurries
tobimas', tobu jumps; flies
tobira a door of a gate
toboshii scarce, meager, scanty
tobu (tobimas') jumps; flies
tōbun for the time being
tōchaku arrival
tochi ground; a piece of land

235

tochū on the way

tōdai 1. lighthouse 2. (T) Tokyo University

toden Tokyo streetcar service ⌈reports

todokemas', todokeru 1. delivers 2. notifies,

todokimas', todoku reaches; arrives

todomarimas', todomaru it stops; it remains

todomemas', todomeru stops it

todorokimas', todoroku roars, rumbles

toei metropolitan (run by the metropolis of

tōfu bean curd ⌊Tokyo)

togamemas', togameru blames, reproves, finds fault with

togarashimas', togarasu sharpens, points

togarimas', togaru gets sharp (pointed)

toge thorn

tōge mountain pass

togemas', togeru achieves, accomplishes

togimas', togu grinds, sharpens, polishes

tōhyō ballot, vote

tōi far-off, distant

toimas', tou inquires

toire(tto) toilet

tōka 10 days; 10th day

tokai city, town

tokashimas', tokasu melts (dissolves) it

tokei clock; watch

tōkei statistics ⌈undone; gets solved

tokemas', tokeru it melts (dissolves); comes

toki time

tōki 1. pottery, ceramics 2. registration

tokimas', toku 1. undoes, unties; solves 2. explains, persuades, preaches 3. combs

tokkuri saké bottle

tokkyū special express (train)

toko bed

tokonoma alcove in Japanese room ⌈time

tokoro 1. place 2. address 3. circumstance,

toku[1] 1. virtue 2. profit, advantage, gain

toku[2] (**tokimas'**) 1. undoes, unties; solves 2. explains, persuades, preaches 3. combs

toku[3] special

tokubetsu special, particular, extra

tokui 1. pride 2. specialty 3. customer

toku-nitō special 2nd class

tokushoku special feature, characteristic

tokushu (**tokyū**) special, particular

tōkyoku the authorities ⌈overnight

tomarimas', tomaru 1. it stops 2. stays

tombo dragonfly ⌈person up overnight

tomemas', tomeru 1. stops it 2. puts a

tomimas', tomu is rich in

tomma idiot, fool

tomo together; company; friend

...to mo! Of course...

tomonaimas', tomonau accompanies

tōmorokoshi corn

tomoshimas', tomosu burns (a light)

tomu (**tomimas'**) is rich in

237

tonaemas', tonaeru advocates; shouts; recites; calls; claims

tōnan southeast

tonari next-door, neighbor(ing) ⌐shocking

tonde-mo-nai, (tonda) outrageous, terrible,

ton-katsu breaded pork cutlet

to-ni-kaku nevertheless

toppatsu outbreak

tora tiger

toraemas', toraeru catches, seizes

torakku 1. truck 2. track

torampu playing cards

tori 1. chicken 2. bird

tori- VERB PREFIX: takes and...

... tōri just as ... ⌐thing)

tōri avenue; passage; way (of doing something)

tori-atsukaimas', -atsukau handles, deals

tori-awase assortment ⌊with

tori-hiki transaction, deal, business

torii gate to a Shinto shrine

tori-keshimas', -kesu cancels, revokes

torimas', toru takes; takes away

tōrimas', tōru passes by, passes through; penetrates ⌐3. agency 4. transmit

toritsugi 1. answering the door 2. an usher

tōrō a stone lantern

tōroku registration

tōron debate, discussion

toru (torimas') takes; takes sway

238

tōru (tōrimas') passes by, passes through; penetrates

Toruko (-buro) Turkey; Turkish (bath)

toshi[1] 1. age 2. year

toshi[2] city

tōshimas', tōsu lets through (in), admits; shows in; pierces, penetrates

toshi-shita younger

... to sh'te (shite) as, by way of

toshi-ue older

toshiyori an old person

tosho-kan library (building)

tosho-shitsu library (room) ⌈(mulled wine)

toso spiced saké drunk at New Year's

tōsu (tōshimas') lets through (in), admits; shows in; pierces, penetrates

to(t)temo terribly, extremely, completely

totonoemas', totonoeru regulates, adjusts; prepares

totonoimas', totonou is in order; is ready

totsuzen suddenly

totte handle

... ni totte for, to

totte kimas' (kuru) brings

totte ikimas' (iku) takes

tou (toimas') inquires

tōwaku embarrassment, dilemma

Tōyō the East, the Orient

to yū which says; which is (called), called

tozan mountain climbing

tōzen naturally; proper. deserved

tsū authority, expert

tsuba spit, saliva

tsubaki camellia

tsubame swallow (bird)

tsubasa wing

tsubo 1. jar 2. 6 sq. ft. ⌈is shut

tsubomarimas', tsubomaru is puckered up;

tsubomemas', tsubomeru puckers it up;

tsubomi flower bud ⌊shuts

tsubu grain; drop ⌈es)

tsuburemas', tsubureru it collapses (smash-

tsubushimas', tsubusu smashes (crushes) it

tsuchi 1. earth, ground 2. hammer

tsūchi report, notice

tsue cane, walking stick

tsuge boxwood

tsugemas', tsugeru tells, informs

tsugi 1. next; following 2. patch

tsugimas', tsugu 1. pours 2. patches 3. in-
herits, succeeds to 4. joins, grafts, glues

tsugi-me joint, seam

tsugi-tsugi one after another ⌈nity

tsugō circumstances, convenience, opportu-

tsui¹ 1. just now 2. unintentionally

tsui² a pair

tsuide 1. opportunity, convenience 2. order

tsuihō purge

tsui-ni at last; after all

...ni tsuite about, concerning

tsūji 1. bowel activity 2. effect

tsūjimas', tsūjiru gets through; communicates; transmits; connects, runs; is understood; is well versed in

...o tsūjite through the good offices of...

tsūjō usual, ordinary

tsuka 1. mound 2. hilt

tsukaemas'[1], **tsukaeru** serves; is useful

tsukaemas',[2] **tsukaeru** is obstructed, clogged up, busy

tsukai, ts'kai 1. message, errand 2. messenger, errand boy

tsukaimas', tsukau uses; spends; employs, handles

tsukamimas', tsukamu seizes, grasps

tsukaremas', tsukareru gets tired

tsukemono pickles

tsukemas', tsukeru 1. attaches, sticks on, adds; turns on (lights); puts on, wears; applies 2. pickles; soaks

tsuki, ts'ki moon

tsukiai association, social company, friend-ship

tsukı-aimas', -au associates with, enjoys the company of

tsuki-atarimas', -ataru runs into; comes to the end of

tsuki-dashimas', -dasu makes protrude, sticks it out

tsuki-demas', -deru protrudes, sticks out

241

tsukimas',[1] **tsukiru** comes to an end, runs out

tsukimas',[2] **tsuku** comes in contact; sticks to; joins; follows; touches; arrives; burns, is on

tsukimas',[3] **tsuku** stabs, thrusts, pushes

tsukurimas', tsukuru makes; builds; writes

tsukuroimas', tsukurou repairs, mends

tsukushimas', tsukusn exhausts, runs out of; exerts oneself, strives

tsuma wife   ⌈marizes

tsumamimas', tsumamu pinches, picks; sum-

tsumamimono things to nibble on (with one's fingers) while drinking

tsumaranai worthless, no good

tsumari after all; in short

tsumarimas', tsumaru is clogged up, choked; is stuck; is shortened; is crammed

tsumbo deaf

tsume claw, nail, hoof

tsumemas', tsumeru stuffs, crams; cans

tsumetai cold (to the touch)

tsumi crime, sin, guilt, fault

tsumimas', tsumu 1. piles it up, accumulates it; deposits; loads 2. gathers, plucks,

tsumori expectation, intention   ⌊clips

tsuna rope. cord, cable

tsunagimas', tsunagu connects, links, ties

tsune usual, ordinary

242

tsuno horn (of an animal)

tsura face

tsurai painful, cruel

tsure company, companion ⌐panied by

tsuremas', tsureru brings along, is accom-

tsuri 1. (small) change 2. fishing

tsuriai balance, equilibrium, symmetry

tsurigane temple bell

tsurimas', tsuru[1] 1. hangs 2. fishes

tsūro passage, thoroughfare

tsuru[2] 1. vine 2. earpieces of glasses frame 3. string (of bow or violin) 4. handle

tsūshin correspondence ; news

tsutaemas', tsutaeru passes it on to some-one else ; reports, communicates ; trans-mits ; hands down

tsutawarimas', tsutawaru is passed on (reported, communicated, transmitted, handed down)

tsutomemas', tsutomeru 1. is employed, works 2. exerts oneself, strives

tsutsu cylinder, pipe ; gun

tsutsumi 1. package, bundle 2. dike, em-bankment

tsutsumimas', tsutsumu wraps it up

tsutsushimi prudence, discretion

tsuttsukimas', tsuttsuku pecks at

tsuya gloss, shine

tsūyaku interpreter ; interpreting

tsuyoi strong; brave

tsuyu 1. dew 2. rainy season 3. light soup

tsuzukemas', tsuzukeru continues it

tsuzukimas', tsuzuku it continues

tsuzumemas', tsuzumeru reduces, cuts down, summarizes

tsuzurimas', tsuzuru 1. spells 2. composes, writes 3. patches; binds; sews (together)

U

u cormorant (fishing bird)

ubaimas', ubau seizes, robs, plunders

uchi 1. house, home; family 2. inside; among

uchi- VERB PREFIX : hits and, takes and

uchiki shy, timid

uchimas', utsu strikes, hits; sends a tele-

uchiwa a flat fan ⌊gram; fires, shoots

ude arm

ude-kubi wrist

ude-wa bracelet

udon Japanese noodles

ue above, upper; on, on top of

ueki-ya gardener

uemas', ueru 1. plants, grows 2. starves

ugokashimas', ugokasu moves it

ugokimas', ugoku it moves

uguisu nightingale

uji family, clan ; family name

ukabimas', ukabu floats

ukagaimas', ukagau 1. visits 2. asks a question 3. hears 4. looks for

ukai 1. cormorant fishing 2. detour

ukemas', ukeru receives; accepts; takes;

uke-tori receipt ⌊gets ; suffers

uke-tsuke information desk ; receptionist

ukimas', uku floats

ukkari absentmindedly

uma horse

umai 1. tasty, delicious 2. skillful, good 3. successful ; profitable

umaremas', umareru is born

ume plum tree

ume-boshi pickled plum

umemas', umeru buries ; fills up ; plugs

umi 1. sea 2. pus

umimas', umu 1. gives birth to 2. festers

ummei destiny

umpan transportation

un fate, luck ⌈(on)

unagashimas', unagasu stimulates, urges

unagi eel

unazukimas', unazuku nods ⌈athletics

undō 1. movement 2. exercise ; sports ;

undō-ba, (-jō) gymnasium ; athletic field

unga canal

unsō transportation

unten operation, running, working, driving
unten-shu driver, operator
uo fish
ura[1] back (side); lining; what's behind it; [the alley
ura[2] bay
ura-girimas', -giru betrays
ura-guchi back door
urami grudge, resentment, ill will
uranai fortunetelling; fortuneteller
uremas', ureru it sells, is in demand; thrives; is popular
ureshii delightful, pleasant, wonderful
uri melon
uri-dashi (special) sale
uri-kake credit sales
uriko shopgirl; salesman; peddler; newsboy
urimas', uru sells
urimono something for sale
uru wool
urusai annoying
urushi lacquer
usagi rabbit
ushi cow, cattle
ushiro behind; (in) back
uso lie, fib
usu mortar
usui thin, pale, weak
uta song; poem
utagaimas', utagau doubts

utaimas', utau sings; recites

utsu (uchimas') strikes, hits; sends a telegram; fires, shoots

utsukushii beautiful

utsurimas'. utsuru 1. it moves, shifts, changes 2. is reflected, can be seen (through); is becoming

utsushimas', utsusu 1. moves (transfers) it; infects, gives another person a disease 2. copies; takes a picture of; projects a picture

utsuwa 1. receptacle 2. tool 3. ability

uttaemas', uttaeru accuses, sues

uttōshii gloomy, dismal

uwabaki slippers

uwabe surface; outer appearances

uwa-gaki address

uwagi coat, jacket

uwagoto raving, delirium

uwaki fickle

uwasa rumor, gossip

uyamaimas', uyamau reveres, respects

W

wa circle; wheel; link; ring; loop

... wa as for (DE-EMPHASIZES PRECEDING [WORD)

wa- Japanese

wabi apology

247

wabishii miserable ; lonely

wadai topic of conversation

wa-fuku, wa-f'ku Japanese clothes

waga-mama selfish

wairo bribery ; graft

waisetsu obscenity

waishatsu shirt

wakai young

wakaremas', wakareru they part, separate :
  it branches off, splits

wakarimas', wakaru it is clear (understood);
  understands ; has good sense

wakashimas', wakasu boils it ⌈stance

wake 1. reason 2. meaning 3. case, circum-

wakemas', wakeru divides (splits, distributes) it ; separates them

waki side (of the chest) ⌈springs forth

wakimas', waku[1] 1. it boils 2. it gushes

waku[2] 1. frame ; crate 2. reel

wakuchin vaccine

wampaku naughty

wan 1. bowl 2. bay

wana trap, lasso

wani crocodile, alligator

wanisu varnish

wan-wan bow-wow !

wappu allotment, instalment

wara rice straw

waraimas', warau laughs

248

ware oneself ; me

waremas', wareru it cracks, it splits

ware-ware we ; us ⌐relatively

wariai rate, percentage ; comparatively,

waribiki discount

wari-kan going Dutch ; splitting the bill

wari-mae share, portion ⌐it

warimas', waru divides it, breaks it, dilutes

warui 1. bad 2. at fault

waru-kuchi(-guchi) abuse, scolding, slander

wasabi horseradish

washi 1. eagle 2. Japanese paper

wa-shoku Japanese food

wasuremono 1. leaving something behind
2. a thing left behind

wasuremas', wasureru forgets ⌐testines

wata 1. cotton 2. (=**hara-wata**) guts, in-

wata-ire cotton-padded (garment)

watakushi, watashi I, me

watarimas', wataru crosses over

watashi-bune ferryboat

watashimas', watasu hands over, ferries

watashi-tachi we, us

Y

ya arrow

...ya and ; or

yā hi !, hello !

249

yabai dangerous (will get you into trouble)

yaban barbarian

yabo stupid ; rustic

yabu bush, thicket

yaburemas', yabureru it tears, bursts; is frustrated

yaburimas', yaburu tears (bursts) it; frustrates ; violates ; defeats

yachin house rent

yado (-ya) inn

yaei camp, bivouac

yagai out in the country, out doors, in the field

yagate before long ; in time

yagi goat

yagu bedclothes ; over-quilt

yahari also ; either ; all the same

yaiba blade ; sword

yaji heckling

yakamashii noisy ; annoying ; over-strict

yakan teakettle

yake desperation

yakedo burn, scald (on the skin)

yakemas', yakeru it burns ; it is baked

yaki- roast (toasts) it ; is jealous

yakimas', yaku burns it ; bakes (roasts,

yaki-mochi 1. jealousy 2. toasted rice-cake

yakimono pottery

yaki-pan toast

yakkai trouble, bother

yakkyoku pharmacy

yaku[1] **(yakimas')** burns it; bakes (roasts, toasts) it; is jealous

yaku[2] approximately, about ⌈use, service

yaku[3] 1. office, post, duty 2. part, role 3.

yakuhin drugs; chemicals

yakume duty, function

yakunin government official

yakusho government office

yakuza no-good, worthless; coarse

yakuzai pharmaceuticals, medicines

yakyū baseball

yama 1. mountain 2. heap, pile 3. climax 4. speculation, venture

yamashii ashamed *or* guilty-feeling

yama-te, yamano-te uptown: the bluff area

Yamato Japan

yamemas', yameru stops it; abolishes; abstains from; gives up; resigns, quits

yami 1. darkness 2. disorder 3. black-marketing 4. anything illicit

yamimas', yamu it stops

yamome widow

yamu-o-enai unavoidable

yanagi willow

yane roof

yaoya greengrocer, vegetable market

yappashi also; either; all the same

...yara ... or something; what with ...

yari spear

251

yarimas', yaru 1. gives 2. sends 3. does

yarō scoundrel, so-and-so!

yasai vegetables

yasashii gentle ; easy

yasemas', yaseru gets thin

yashi coconut

yashin ambition; treachery ⌐nourishes

yashinaimas', yashinau brings up, rears;

yasui 1. cheap 2. easy 3. likely to, apt to

yasumi rest, break ; vacation ; holiday

yasumimas', yasumu rests, takes time off ;
stays away (from school) ; goes to bed,

yatoimas', yatou employs, hires ⌊sleeps

yatsu guy, fellow, wretch ; thing

yatto at last ; barely, with difficulty

yattsu eight

yawarakai soft, mild

yaya a little ; a little while

yayakoshii complicated ; puzzling ; tangled

yo 1. the world at large, the public 2. the
age, the times ; one's lifetime 3. night

yo- four

yō[1] manner, way ; kind, sort

...no yō like, as if ; seems like

yō[2] **(go-yō)** 1. business 2. use, service 3.

yō[3] gist ⌊going to bathroom

yō- Western ; American

yobi reserve ⌐2. invites

yobimas', yobu 1. calls ; names ; summons

252

yobō precaution, prevention

yochi room, space, margin, leeway

yōdo iodine

yōfuku, yōf'ku (Western-style) clothes; a suit; a dress

yōfuku-ya tailor; clothing shop

yogoremas', yogoreru gets soiled (dirty)

yogoshimas', yogosu soils, dirties, stains

yōgu tools, implements

yōhin imported goods

yohō forecast, prediction

yohodo considerably, a good deal

yoi[1] evening

yoi[2] = **ii** good

yōi preparation; caution

yōiku bringing up, education

yoimas', you gets drunk; gets seasick

yōji 1. business, errand 2. toothpick 3. infant

yōjin precaution, caution, care

yōka 8 days; 8th day

yoke protection, shelter, screen

yokei superfluous, unnecessary, uncalled for

yokemas', yokeru avoids, keeps away from

yōki cheerful, bright, lively

yokin deposit (of money), bank account

yokka 4 days; 4th day

yoko width; sidewise

yokochō sidestreet, alley

yoko-girimas', -giru crosses, cuts across, intersects

yoku[1] greed

253

yoku[2] 1. well 2. lots, much 3. lots, often

yoku- the next (day, etc.)

yokubarimas', yokubaru is greedy

yōkyū demand, claim, request

yo-mawari night watchman

yome bride

yomimas', yomu reads

yōmō wool

yon four

yondokoro-nai inevitable

yo-nin 4 people

yopparaimas', yopparau gets drunk

yoppodo considerably, a good deal

...yori that; from; since   ⌈3. meet

yorimas', yoru 1. drops in 2. comes near

yorokobimas', yorokobu is happy, delighted

yoron public opinion

Yōroppa Europe

yoroshii very well; excellent ⌈best wishes

yoroshiku, yorosh'ku one's regards, one's

Dōzo yoroshiku. How do you do.

yoru[1] night   ⌈3. meet

yoru[2] (**yorimas'**) 1. drops in 2. comes near

yosan budget, estimate

yōsan raising silkworms, silk farming

yosemas', yoseru 1. lets approach, brings
  near 2. collects, gathers 3. adds 4. sends

Yosh'! OK!   ⌊5. makes (a crease)

yoshi reason; meaning; circumstance; means

yōshi forms, blanks, papers ⌈ing

yōshoku foreign (Western, American) cook-

yoshu foreign liquor

yoso somewhere else; alien, strange

yosō expectation, presumption

yoshimas', yosu stops it

yōsu circumstances; aspect; appearance, look

yotamono hoodlum

yō-tashi business, errand

yotei expectation, plan

yōten gist, point

...ni yotte according to; because of

yottsu four

you (yoimas') gets drunk; gets seasick

yowai weak; frail; easily intoxicated

yoyaku reservation, subscription, booking

yōyaku gradually; at last; barely

yoyū room, leeway, margin, excess, surplus

yu (o-yu) hot water, bath; hot tea

'yū (iimas') says; *see also* to yū

yūbe last night

yubi finger; toe

yūbi elegant, graceful

yūbin mail

yūbin-kyoku post office

yubinuki thimble

yubiwa ring

yubi-zan finger counting

yubune bathtub

255

yūdachi a sudden shower

yudan negligence, carelessness, remissness

yudanemas', yudaneru entrusts, commits

Yudaya-jin Jew

Yudaya-kyō Judaism

yue reason, grounds

yūkan evening paper

yuki snow

...-yuki bound for

yukkuri slowly; at ease

yūkō effective, valid

yuku = iku goes

yume dream

yūmei famous

yumi bow (for archery)

yumi-gata curve, arch, bow

yūmoa humor, wit

yunyū import(ing)

yūran excursion

yūrei ghost

yuremas', yureru it shakes, sways, rocks, rolls

yūretsu 1. quality 2. boldness

yuri lily

yūri profitable, advantageous

yurimas', yuru shakes it

yurui loose, slack; lax, lenient; slow

yurushimas', yurusu allows, permits, lets; pardons, forgives

yūryoku strong, powerful, influential

yūshō victory, championship
yūshoku supper
yūshū melancholy
yushutsu export(ing)
yusō transport(ation)
yusuri blackmail, extortion
yutaka abundant, plentiful ; wealthy
yutte saying ; says and
yūutsu melancholy, gloom
yuwakashi teakettle
yūwaku temptation ; seduction
yuzu orange ⌜cedes ; is inferior
yuzurimas', yuzuru gives up ; gives in ;

Z

za 1. theater 2. seat
zabuton cushion to sit on
zadan chat
zai 1. lumber 2. material 3. talent 4. wealth
zai- (resident) in
zaibatsu the big financial groups
zaidan a foundation (philanthropical, etc.)
zaikai financial circles
zaimoku lumber, wood
zairu a mountain-climbing rope
zairyō raw material
zaisan property
zaisei finance

zakka miscellaneous goods, sundries
zambō slander
zange confession (of sins)
zankoku cruel, brutal
zannen regret, disappointed ; too bad
zara-ni found everywhere, very common
zara-zara rough
zaseki seat
zashiki room, living room
zasshi magazine, periodical
zassō weeds
zatsu- miscellaneous ; rough ; coarse
zatto roughly ; briefly
zehi 1. without fail, for sure 2. right or
zei tax, customs ⌊wrong
zeikan customs, custom house
zeikin tax
zeitaku luxury, extravagance
zembu all
zemmai 1. spring, hairspring 2· fern
zemmen 1. the entire surface 2. the front
zemmetsu annihilation ⌊side
zempō the front
zen- all, total, complete, the whole
zentai the whole body, the entirety
zento the future, prospects
zen-ya the night before ⌈gether
zenzen completely, utterly, entirely, alto-
zeppeki precipice

---

zerii jelly

zetsubō despair

zettai absolute(ly)

zō[1] statue, image, portrait

zō[2] elephant

zōdai enlargement, increase

zōgan inlaid work ; damascene

zōge ivory

zōho supplement

zōka increase, growth

zoku[1] common, vulgar ; popular

zoku[2] rebel ; thief

zokugo slang

zoku-shimas', -suru belongs ⌈succession

zokuzoku one right after another, in rapid

zombun as much as one likes

zongai beyond expectations

zōni rice-cakes boiled with vegetables (eaten at New Year's)

zonjimas', zonjiru thinks, feels ; knows

zonzai slovenly, rough, careless, sloppy

zōri straw sandals

zorozoro in a queue, all lined up

zōsen ship building

zōshin promotion, betterment, increase

zōsho book collection, library

zotto with a shiver (of horror)

zu picture, drawing, map, diagram

zuan sketch, design

259

zubon trousers, pants

zubon-shita underpants, shorts

zuhyō chart, diagram

zuibun 1. fairly, rather 2. quite, extremely

zuihitsu essays

zuii voluntary, optional

zukai illustration, diagram

-zuki a lover of ..., a great ... fan

zukku canvas; duck

zukku-kutsu tennis shoes

zunō brains, head

zuremas', zureru slips out of place, gets loose

zurosu panties; drawers

zuru cheating

zurui sly, cunning, tricky

... zutsu each, apiece

zutsū headache

zutto 1. directly 2. by far, much (more) 3. all through, all the time

zuzan sloppy, slipshod, careless

zūzūshii brazen, shameless, pushy

PART III

Writing Charts

NOTE: The following charts show the essentials of *kana* spelling. The squarish letters on the left are *katakana*, which is used to write foreign words and odd-sounding native words. The roundish letters on the right are the ones used for other words. In addition, modern Japanese use about 2000 characters of Chinese origin, called *kanji*. The first two charts show the simple syllables; the third shows those with the -y- element inserted. After these are notes on special combinations, such as long vowels and consonants. The Romanization in heavy black type is that used in this book. For some of the syllables, there are other ways of Romanizing them, and these are also shown, but in regular typeface.

あ ア a	か カ ka	さ サ sa	た タ ta	な ナ na	は ハ ha	ま マ ma	や ヤ ya	ら ラ ra	わ ワ wa	ん ン -n-m
い イ i	き キ ki k'	し シ shi sh' si	ち チ chi ch' ti	に ニ ni	ひ ヒ hi	み ミ mi	—	り リ ri	ゐ ヰ (wi)	
う ウ u	く ク ku k'	す ス su s'	つ ツ tsu ts' tu	ぬ ヌ nu	ふ フ fu f' hu	む ム mu	ゆ ユ yu	る ル ru	—	
え エ e	け ケ ke	せ セ se	て テ te	ね ネ ne	へ ヘ he	め メ me	—	れ レ re	ゑ ヱ (we)	
お オ o	こ コ ko	そ ソ so	と ト to	の ノ no	ほ ホ ho	も モ mo	よ ヨ yo	ろ ロ ro	を ヲ (wo)	

ガ が ga	キ ぎ gi	グ ぐ gu	ゲ げ ge	ゴ ご go
ザ ざ za	ジ じ ji / zi	ズ ず zu	ゼ ぜ ze	ゾ ぞ zo
ダ だ da	ヂ ぢ ji / di	ヅ づ zu / du	デ で de	ド ど do
パ ぱ pa	ピ ぴ pi	プ ぷ pu	ペ ぺ pe	ポ ぽ po
バ ば ba	ビ び bi	ブ ぶ bu	ベ べ be	ボ ぼ bo

キャ kya	シャ sha sya	チャ cha tya	ギャ gya	ジャ ja zya	ヂャ ja dya
キュ kyu	シュ shu syu	チュ chu tyu	ギュ gyu	ジュ ju zyu	ヂュ ju dyu
キョ kyo	ショ sho syo	チョ cho tyo	ギョ gyo	ジョ jo zyo	ヂョ jo dyo

ニャ nya	ヒャ hya	ビャ bya	ピャ pya
ニュ nyu	ヒュ hyu	ビュ byu	ピュ pyu
ニョ nyo	ヒョ hyo	ビョ byo	ピョ pyo

ミャ mya	リャ rya
ミュ myu	リュ ryu
ミョ myo	リョ ryo

Long vowels are usually shown by re-
peating the vowel when writing in hiragana:
ā ああ, kā かあ, ū うう, fū ふう, ii いい,
nii にい, ē ええ, tē てえ.

In katakana, a single long stroke is often
used (especially for foreign words):
ā アー, kā カー, ū ウー, fū フー, ii イー,
nii ニー, e エー, tē テー.

But in hiragana the long ō is usually
written as if it were **ou** (for most, but not
all, words):
ō おう, kō こう, sō そう, kyō きょう, yō
よう

Long consonants (**pp, tt, tch, kk, ss,
ssh**) are written by inserting **tsu,** usually
written smaller than the other letters:
kippu きっぷ, **natte** なって, **botchan** ボッ
チャン, **gakkō** がっこう, **massugu** マッスグ,
issho いっしょ.

But long **-mm-** and **-nn-** are written with
ん and the appropriate symbol from the **ma**
or **na** columns:
ammari あんまり, **semmon** センモン, **annai**
あんない, **san-nen** さんねん, **sam-myaku** さ
んみゃく.

266